DOING GOOD

WITH OTHER PEOPLE'S MONEY

DOING GOOD

WITH OTHER PEOPLE'S MONEY

The Essential Guide to Winning Grants and Contracts

RICK STEINER, PH.D.

Hatherleigh Press is committed to preserving and protecting the natural resources of the earth. Environmentally responsible and sustainable practices are embraced within the company's mission statement.

Visit us at www.hatherleighpress.com and register online for free offers, discounts, special events, and more.

DOING GOOD WITH OTHER PEOPLE'S MONEY

CONTENTS

CHAPTER 1

Doing Good with Other People's Money

*D*oing *Good with Other People's Money* (DGWOPM) is about "the Doers." The millions of nonprofits, faith-based organizations, schools, colleges, universities, philanthropists, foundations, corporations, state and local governments of every type and stripe who see the world as it should and could be, not as it is. Those wanting to make Planet Earth a better, safer, fairer, healthier, and more hospitable place for all, regardless of wealth, position, race, or gender. Those who want to be part of the solution, not the problem by successfully navigating the highly competitive and oftentimes complex and confusing world of identifying, applying for and winning grants and contracts from government, foundations, and corporations.

Now retired, after working in University for some 40 years as a senior university official, active grant writer, project director and trainer, I was awarded some $500 million in grants and contracts from government, corporations, and foundations. Some of those projects are still operating and being funded today, some twenty years later. It's time for me to pass on what I have learned to the next generation of those wanting to "Do Good with Other People's Money."

Doing Good with Other People's Money walks you through the entire grant- and contract-seeking process by providing the knowledge, tactics, strategies, and insights necessary for building financially self-sustaining grant- and contract-centric enterprises

Competing for and winning grants and contracts isn't about bragging rights, or "we won and you lost." It's not even about the money. It is about what the money will do. Whether you are a novice or a seasoned grant-getting warrior, there is always more to learn, because funding priorities are always changing, grant and contract processes constantly evolving, new competitors always arriving, and catastrophic events always happening. The information provided in the book will dramatically increase your chances for funding success by helping grant seekers avoid the common pitfalls so many novices stumble over in their initial grant-seeking efforts. So, let's get down to business—the business of *Doing Good with Other People's Money*.

WHAT THIS BOOK IS ABOUT

IT'S ABOUT DONORS: The many governments, foundations, corporations, and philanthropists with deep pockets who fund all this Good-Deed-Doing and who want to make the world a better place for all.

IT'S ABOUT DOERS: The millions of nonprofits, faith-based organizations, schools, and colleges that work to do good. It's about the Mother Teresa's, the everyday heroes joining in common cause to make the world a better place.

IT'S ABOUT DISRUPTORS: The truth-tellers who aren't afraid to say, "The king has no clothes on." The sorts of people who aren't content to stand on the sidelines and take what comes; they recognize the issues in the world around them, call them out, and work towards a solution.

IT'S ABOUT THE DISTRESSED: Those who don't know where their next meal is coming from, those who've been left by the side of life's road, who no longer have the will or capacity to make life better for themselves.

IT'S ABOUT making the world a better place for all.

IT'S ABOUT you and me, as well as our families, friends, neighbors, and communities, working together to secure the future for the next generation, making sure they inherit our accomplishments and not our problems.

IT'S ABOUT the "haves" and the "have not's," and giving people a hand-up instead of a handout. It's about creating vibrant, safe, caring and healthy communities and about affordable housing.

IT'S ABOUT every child's right, regardless of their family's financial circumstances, to attend quality schools and have access to a college education.

IT'S ABOUT ending intergenerational poverty and children having children. It's about job security and job opportunities for all, with equal access to the training needed to get and keep jobs.

IT'S ABOUT having access to quality medical care, regardless of where we live or how much money we have. It's about ending dependency on government handouts by teaching self-sufficiency and accepting personal responsibility for shaping our own futures.

IT'S ABOUT equality of opportunity, not outcomes, and teaching people how to succeed. It's about helping those who went down the wrong roads to find the right ones and about leaving no one behind.

More importantly, it's about handing the baton to the next generations of those wanting to *do good with other people's money*.

DGWOPM will teach you how to:

- Establish the legal, administrative, and infrastructure for making your nonprofit, faith-based organization, school, college, or university contract- and/or grant-eligible

- Build the requisite programmatic infrastructure necessary to deliver effective services in your chosen area(s) of endeavor

- Identify critical pathways and decision points to funding success

- Evaluate and select "best-fit" grant-getting strategies and approaches consistent with your organization's culture, capability, and mission

- Diversify your base of financial and programmatic support through strategic alliances

- Create a positive track record and reputation

- Successfully re-invent yourselves when funding priorities change

- Establish positive sponsor relationships by attending meetings and familiarizing yourselves with their funding priorities, interests, and strategies

- Play by sponsor's rules, not yours

- Decipher the protocols sponsors use to review, score, and select winning proposals and how to use that knowledge to your advantage

- Administer and manage your grant and contact portfolio consistent with sponsor requirements

- Identify critical pathways and decision points to funding success by evaluating best-fit grant-getting strategies

- Diversify your base of financial and programmatic support through strategic alliances

- Above all, **how to *write winning proposals***

CHAPTER 2

How Grant Giving and Getting Began

Most of us "want to do good," seeking to make the world a better place for ourselves, for our families, our children, for our communities, and for the world at large. We do this through everyday kindness, by donating to worthy causes, by engaging in collective endeavors, or by volunteering our time to a myriad of purposes and causes. While some have more to give than others, be it money or of themselves, our worth should not be judged or measured by how much money and "things" we have.

Some are fortunate enough to become the next generation of philanthropists and financial supporters of good deeds. Others pursue the helping professions or work in government, striving to make a difference in the lives of others. Still others share their joy, knowledge, and wise counsel to make our world a better place for all by holding a personal vision of the world as it should be and not as it is.

A COLLECTIVE OBLIGATION

Yet all those good intentions and random kindnesses on their own are not enough. There is too much pain and suffering in our world for one person—or a nation, for that matter—to solve everything alone. That is why people like myself make their life's work out of doing good with *other* people's money. So, welcome to my world, where people of good intention, great energy, and passion strive to make our communities a better place to live and work. I was there at the start of the modern era of big government, when it finally dawned on our political and business elites that our country was splitting, sadly along racial lines. Generations of turning a blind eye to poverty, misery, and inequality was inexorably eating at the moral and social structure of our society. This set the stage for decades of violence, strife, and conflict beginning in the 1960's and becoming even more virulent today.

I learned much on the front lines of the poverty program. I had the privilege of helping communities, governments, and even nations become better stewards of their people and their resources, despite the challenges of this fractious world. I was there as America struggled to redefine its core values—that everyone has worth and that all peoples have the same inherent rights, regardless of color or economic standing and to participate in the American Dream. At that time in history, the battle ground in the national debate revolved around the role government should take in the national renaissance of "inclusion." Our national leaders assumed that money was the answer. Hastily, they created new bureaucracies dedicated to ending poverty and inequality and creating a fairer and more inclusive society. Unfortunately, this did not work. Being in the heart of the beast, I can tell you unequivocally that it did not; rather, it fueled the fires, both literally and figuratively.

AMERICA OPENS ITS DOORS TO THE WORLD

In late 19th and early 20th century America, the demand for labor greatly exceeded its supply. America opened its doors to the world and to mass immigration. Cities could not easily cope with this flood of new immigrants coming from different cultures and speaking different languages. Overcrowding was the inevitable result as a flood of immigrants piled extended families into small and unsanitary cold-water flats. Tainted food and water, poor hygiene, and the general unsanitary conditions predictably led to disease and epidemics.

All the while, government at every level remained on the sidelines. The care of the poor, the sick, and the needy was left to relatives, friends, church congregations, fraternal societies, neighbors, the Salvation Army, and local residents. Our governments remained aloof and above the fray of everyday living in these newly-forming ghettos.

THE GREAT DEPRESSION: ROOSEVELT CHANGES EVERYTHING

It was the Great Depression, set off by the market crash of 1929, that changed the course of our nation's future. Depending on your personal perspective or what history book you read, President Roosevelt's "alphabet soup" of laws and executive orders that comprised The New Deal either saved America or were the progenitors of the modern American Welfare State. While Roosevelt's efforts were effective in bringing hope to people that had none, it did not bring America out of the Depression. Rather, it was the run-up to World War II which jump-started the nation's factories, farms, coal mines, oil wells, steel producers, auto manufacturers, ship yards, railroads, and any company that could transition its factories to produce war goods that ultimately put Americans back to work.

FIRE IN THE STREETS

With the ending of World War II, America went back to doing what it did best: taking care of business rather than taking care of people. The 50's were relatively calm, with limited social progress. The 60's, however was a time of dramatic change and redefinition. The 1960's proved to be a transformative decade in the life of our country and its people and institutions. The confluence of the Civil Rights Movement, the Vietnam War, the assassinations of President Kennedy, Martin Luther King, Jr., and Robert Kennedy, the heating up of the Cold War, and the recognition that tens of millions of people were living in abject poverty, forced our government out of its post-World War II apathy. The youth found their voice, while government at every level failed to listen until the country literally started to burn.

The wake-up call came like a smack across the head when riots erupted in Harlem in 1964 and Watts in 1965. I was working in Harlem on July 16, 1964, as a summer physical education teacher when a young black man was shot by a New York City police officer in front of his friends and dozens of witnesses, setting off six nights of rioting, vandalism, and looting. The Harlem Riot was the precursor to other riots around the country and preceded the infamous Watts Riot and conflagration of 1965, which set our country in a new and uncharted direction.

The inner cities with their grinding poverty, failed schools, joblessness, deplorable housing, and burgeoning youth populations across the country were powder kegs waiting for the fuse to be lit. Watts, a dramatically poor inner-city enclave near Los Angeles, proved to be the tinder box that would set off a cascade of riots around the country. The infamous Watts Riot, ignited over a minor incident when two black youths were arrested for drunk driving by two white police officers, escalated into a youth-driven uprising that left Watts in ruins, with thirty-four people killed and thousands more wounded. All of America turned on their televisions, as I did, and watched the city burn. Americans were educated and appalled, angry, and then sensitized to the poverty that had been hidden from their view—that is, until then. Yet, government was slow to react, believing it was just a "one-off"—they were wrong. It was to be repeated in different forms and locations for almost a decade.

This time of racial turmoil ran headlong in to the Vietnam anti-war movement, which, taken together, set our country on a new course. I was an eyewitness not only to the Harlem riot but to the dramatic social upheavals and international events that would shape our country for the next five decades.

President Johnson, an astute politician, was literally thrust into the presidency after the Kennedy assassination. This was a time of crisis for our country; America was literally coming apart at the seams. Race relations and riots, riots and poverty, poverty and urban decay, urban decay and crime twisted together with the growing Civil Rights and Vietnam anti-war movements, contributing to a pervasive sense of hopelessness, confusion, and social disarray. Something had to be done quickly, or the social fabric holding this country together would surely give way.

Existing government organizations and agencies at the federal, state, and local levels were almost paralyzed by the rapidly changing events and youth-led insurgencies confronting our country. Competing social and racial groups all wanted their share of Johnson's "Great Society."

JOHNSON DECLARES WAR ON POVERTY

Johnson's political response to the voices in the streets was his declaration of a "War on Poverty," announced in his State of the Union address on January 8, 1964. For the first time in history, large sums of public money would be sent through unregulated channels to non-governmental community organizations and not-for-profits. The implementing legislation was contained in the Economic Opportunity Act of 1964, which established the Office of Economic Opportunity. Some perceived the new Office of Economic Opportunity as a sop to the poor, while others saw it as a continuation of Roosevelt's New Deal. President Johnson's War on Poverty took our nation in an entirely new direction, one that is still being debated and challenged today. Corruption, abuse, and inefficiency took their toll on these hastily-planned programs. New government bureaucracies emerged and grew to enormous size. Many trace the roots of the burgeoning welfare state and our huge deficits back to Johnson and his "Great Society."

POWER TO THE PEOPLE

Maximum feasible participation by the poor became OEO's battle cry. Its solution to long standing and institutionalized racism and poverty, as witnessed and manifested in the ghettos and inner-city neighborhoods throughout our country. OEO was tasked with the responsibility of redirecting government funding to grassroots organizations. These

neighborhood organizations were to be assisted and guided by politi-
cally-friendly nonprofits and faith-based organizations, including universities, colleges, consultants, and activists of all stripes. Funds flowed
to these yet-untested, nontraditional entities. The political class naively
assumed that papering the streets with money and parachuting in a
new generation of advisers and consultants, also known as community
activists, would miraculously bootstrap communities from desperation
to participation in the American Dream.

MONEY TO THE PEOPLE

The new theory was that the poor and the lower class needed to be
empowered to fully participate in our democracy. Accomplishing this
goal, according to the new Office of Economic Opportunity, could only
be achieved if neighborhood residents had direct involvement in their
personal futures and in the futures of their communities. The mechanism was the establishment and the direct federal funding of a coterie of
new neighborhood and grassroot organizations, directed and controlled
by residents, whose politics and approaches were sometimes hostile to
the established political order. This was the first time in history that
federal tax dollars found their way to nongovernmental organizations.

These three words, *maximum feasible participation,* along with the
inevitable abuse and corruption common to rapidly deployed, ill-con-
sidered government projects, sowed the seeds of discord leading to the
politicization of community action agencies and the demise of the War
on Poverty. How do I know? I was there and I watched it all go down—it
wasn't pretty, I assure you!

A BUREAUCRACY ON STEROIDS: THE ERA OF BIG GOVERNMENT

President Johnson didn't stop at OEO. Indeed, he created his own
alphabet soup of new programs and projects to lift the poor and lower

class out of poverty. The money to fund these new initiatives literally flowed into what was variously referred to as the "mean streets," or the ghetto. Volunteers in Service to America (VISTA), Upward Bound, Head Start, Jobs Corps, College Work Study Programs, Neighborhood Development Centers, and numerous other government-funded and locally-run programs popped up like weeds. Many of these took root and are still operating today.

These initiatives were soon followed by the Food Stamp Act of 1964 and the Elementary and Secondary Education Act of 1965. Direct federal funding of local education was a watershed event, and the first time the national government became directly involved in funding what had previously been a strictly local and state function. These new initiatives were soon followed by The Higher Education Act of 1965, Medicare and Medicaid, the creation of the Department of Housing and Urban Affairs, and a plethora of urban renewal programs giving hope to millions of poor Americans.

Was the war on poverty a success? That's up to each of us to decide. What it did do, however, was send government in new directions. Whether it was the right direction or not is totally dependent on your personal political views.

THE GREAT MONEY CHASE

Grant and contract giving and getting, as we know it today, had its origins in Johnson's War on Poverty. It was the first time in our government's history that significant amounts of federal tax dollars were used to fund entities like nonprofits, community groups, universities, colleges, schools, charities, and foundations generically called Non-Governmental Organizations (NGO's). This provided a host of nongovernmental organizations the opportunity to replace charitable giving, corporate largess, and individual donations (which were hard to come by) with more plentiful and reliable federal dollars, allowing them to expand their reach, their programs, and their value on a local and national scale. How do I know? I was a poverty warrior right out of graduate school at ground zero in Syracuse, New York.

BLOCK GRANTS: A NEW FUNDING MODEL

The era of Block Grants, initiated by President Clinton, which continues today in full force, was also a funding game changer. The beneficiaries to this new largess were the sub-units of government, the states, cities, counties, Indian tribes, nonprofits, school districts, universities, and charities of all types. Whether it was Temporary Aid to Needy Families (TANF), Education Block Grants, Child Care Block Grants, or the dozens of other block grants that found their way to the states, this created "Round 2" of the Great Money Chase. Under this new conceptualization, control over how funds can be expended and who can apply, administer, and expend these funds is totally the state's call.

Federal funding prior to block grants typically bypassed the states. They were formula driven and didn't consider regional, geographical, economic, social, or political differences. They were typically "take it or leave it". Many states left money on the table because of onerous stipulations and federal requirements, or simply because of the mind-bending complexity of federal rules and requirements. At the advent of block grants, the states were in control, which can be good or bad depending on your perspective. If there are overruns, they eat it. If program requirements are met, states can retain unexpended dollars rather than send them back to Washington. This created a huge incentive for the states to find better, more efficient ways to deliver programs, thereby opening-up new funding opportunities for nonprofits, schools, and colleges to participate in the direct delivery of programs. *You see, sometimes history can inform the present.*

CHAPTER 3

Leaving the World Better Than We Found It

O ur evolution to peaceful coexistence has yet to occur. Yet inch by inch, and step by step, many have arrived at the understanding that as we inhabit our world for only a short-time, we are morally obligated to pass it on to the next generation better than we found it. *We want future generations to build on our success, rather than rebuild what we destroyed.*

DOERS, DONORS, DISRUPTORS AND THE DISTRESSED

There are four major players in the world of *Doing Good with Other People's Money*. They are:

DOERS: Those who live, work, and do their good deed doing in a world bounded only by their collective imaginations, pocketbooks, values, and capabilities.

DONORS: The local, state, and federal agencies, foundations, corporations, and local businesses who can provide the priorities, the money, and the insights that make all this good deed doing possible.

THE DISRUPTERS: The change agents, the provocateurs, those who see the world as it should be, not as it is.

THE DISTRESSED: Individuals, groups, cities, communities, the environment, the poor, the sick, the elderly, or disappearing wildlife, who continue to be assaulted by both man and nature.

The Doers

Doers are the "feet on the ground" types. They are the individuals and organizations with the knowledge, human resources, capabilities, and experience to successfully resolve problems, whether caused by man or nature. Doers can be an individual with a personal dream and the desire to make the world better for others; they can be nonprofits, faith-based organizations, schools, museums, neighborhood organizations, hospitals, or just "good deed doers" of all stripes and types wanting to *do good with other people's money*. They are the communities fed up with crime, poverty, violence, and failing schools. They are our fire departments and emergency medical services, who are available 24 hours a day, every day of the year. They are our friends, families, and colleagues, and our local governments. They are you and me. In each of their unique ways, they help to make our world a better, fairer, healthier, and safer place to live.

Success in the world of *Doing Good with Other People's Money* requires Doers to: (a) attract like-minded people who want to join in a common cause, (b) create functioning organizations around their model or vision of this "better place," (c) shape a public constituency by convincing others of the importance and urgency of their cause, and (d) identify clear and convincing pathways to resolving social, environmental, and economic dislocations. More importantly, Doers must secure sufficient monies and cross-organizational commitments to make all this good stuff happen.

The Donors

Donors are the funders, the organizers, the innovators, and the conduit for both temporary and structural change.

The "big dog" is, of course, government, primarily federal departments and agencies. They are the thousands of state and local governments with access to federal funding and locally-sourced dollars. They are the foundations, corporations, and philanthropists who fund and collaborate with Doers in resolving systemic problems. Even more importantly, they are the vehicles for awarding funding to organizations wanting to do good with other people's money.

Donors are typically cause-specific. The mission, interests, and fields of endeavor for government organizations are determined both legislatively and administratively. Private foundations and corporations, however, establish their own funding interests and priorities typically involving leadership, boards of directors, and community members. Working together, Doers and Donors can turn hopes and dreams into opportunities. It is through symbiotic relationships between Donors and Doers that advances can be achieved and life made better for most, if not all.

The Disruptors

Disruptors are the contrarians. They enjoy the stress they create because they truly believe they are right and know more than others. They disrupt because that is what they do— but those disruptions serve a very important role in challenging common wisdom and false expectations. If we aren't challenged, we get lazy and complacent. Some of us have blinders on, purposely not wanting to see or believe that millions of adults and children are homeless and wandering the streets, sleeping in doorways, and eating out of dumpsters.

Disruptors might, at first blush, appear to be the "harbingers of Doom," appearing to bring an end to the comfortable order and false sense of security we enjoy. But we need those voices because we have mastered the art of selective seeing and hearing. Indeed, there is real poverty out there, and it's not only in the inner cities, but in the rural areas of America, as well. Alcoholism, family violence, drug abuse, mental abuse, and hunger are not only restricted to the streets we politely refer to as inner cities; it's in suburbia, as well.

The Distressed

Those who too many choose to ignore. They are the millions of Americans living on the margins of society and in poverty, requiring assistance from others. They are the teenage mothers, people that are food insecure, the poor, the homeless, the school dropouts, the welfare recipients, the emotionally unstable, the substance abusers. They are the progenitors of the next generation of poor who will then repeat the cycle of poverty and dependence with no end in sight

Communities are in distress for a variety of reasons. Some are of their own making, while others are caused by social and economic dislocations, limited job opportunities, unstable and violent neighborhoods, and government and educational malfeasance. Our society is in distress because we have yet to figure out how to get along with each other and create genuine pathways to independence and self-sufficiency.

Above all, the distressed are the children who were brought into this world without their knowledge and consent and who will become the next generation of "hopeless and helpless" unless we are truly prepared, as a nation, to intervene in authentic ways.

DGWOPM IS A TEAM SPORT

While many community-based institutions and organizations have the desire, the capability, and most importantly, local knowledge, they typically don't have ready access to the financial resources needed to turn these good ideas into proven realities. Likewise, Donors are not necessarily aware of the specific problems plaguing our local communities, nor do they have the answers and the delivery capability (because that is not their primary mission). What they do have is the ability, willingness, infrastructure, and, more importantly, the financial assets to make our world a better place.

PRACTICE, PATIENCE, PERSISTENCE, PERFORMANCE AND PROFESSIONALISM

As in all endeavors, it takes *practice, patience, persistence, performance* and *professionalism* for any social intervention to bear fruit. We must be willing to lose if we ever hope to win. We also need to bring something special to the game; that is, confidence. Without confidence, every obstacle appears insurmountable. The learning curve on the road to funding success can be less traumatic if we are prepared for the trip. We need to collectively learn the Rules of the Road: how to interpret complicated grant and contract announcements and how to respond and write compelling proposals. We must also display the behaviors, language, knowledge, and interpersonal skills that successful grant- and contract-getters must bring to the table every time they ask others to support their causes.

Ultimately, our successes are not measured by what we say or how we say it. Rather, our successes are measured by what we do, what we have accomplished, and whether others have benefited from our actions in real measurable terms. Our future successes are built on doing what we said we would or could do—no excuses. It's about turning words into actions. It's about deliverables; not future promises. It's about accomplishment and reputation and solving problems for those who depend on us. It's not about overpromising and under-delivering and saying you'll do better next time, because there won't be a "next time." Always remember: *Good news travels fast, bad news, faster!*

CHAPTER 4

Why Some Succeed Where Others Fail

IT'S NOT ABOUT BEING GOOD, IT'S ABOUT DOING GOOD

If you're reading this book, it's for one primary reason: to make your organization successful in the highly competitive world of grant- and contract-winning. Don't be under the false impression that grant and contract getting is about "being good," because it's really about "doing good." Many altruistic, kind, and caring individuals desperately want to make the world a better place but don't have the faintest idea how to turn hopes and dreams into realities. Whether on the micro or macro scale, they haven't the faintest clue where to begin. So, it's time for a reality check. Who has the "right stuff" to make it in our world, and how do you know what the "right stuff" is, anyway? Well, I'm going to tell you, and that is what this chapter is all about.

DONORS WANT SOLUTIONS—THEY ALREADY KNOW THE PROBLEMS

Let's start with the biggest mistake most novice money seekers make: approaching Donors with an attitude. All too often, over-eager Doers will introduce themselves by railing against the problems of the world.

The unfairness of life, the "haves" and "have not's". They use anger and righteous indignation as a blunt instrument, almost in a threatening manner, to extract money from a potential Donor, and that is neither a good money-getting tactic nor professional way to win friends and influence people. This happened almost daily when I worked in the community action agency. Such confrontational tactics, while successful in the 60's and 70's, no longer work today.

Doing good with other people's money has become highly structured and formalized. Funders are well-aware of the problems our nation confronts: the inequities, the racial divide, the poverty, so they don't have to be verbally abused to understand there are people suffering out there—they know more than you think. You are preaching to the choir.

WHAT DONORS WANT

Donors are looking for innovative or untested solutions that just might work, not recitations about how bad or unfair things are or what amounts to a funding fight between competing organizations, as each tries to one-up the other, insisting that *their* cause is the most pressing and deserving of financial support. Donors often turn to select nonprofits for advice and as grantees because of their positive community reputations and personal knowledge of their capabilities and because they are typically closest to the problems impacting people and communities or geographically proximate to distressed communities.

WHAT WILL YOU BRING TO THE TABLE?

While it might appear counterintuitive, DGWOPM is not about how many people go to sleep hungry every evening, or about how many people are homeless. It's about what your organization brings to the table and how you intend on eliminating all those social, physical, and environmental maladies confronting millions of the less fortunate every day of their lives. Donors are aware of the struggles. Isn't that what *Doing Good with Other People's Money* is about? Isn't that what nonprofits, faith-based organizations, community organizations, and schools are all about? That is, making life better for others, however "better" is defined.

IT'S NOT ABOUT THE MONEY, IT'S ABOUT WHAT THE MONEY WILL DO

It's not about getting money, it is about what the money can do. Sometimes the "getting" feels harder than the "doing." Funders want solutions, not schemes. What they want to fund are practical, cost-effective, and realistic projects, not "pie-in-the-sky" solutions. Doers must not only convince Donors of the value of proposed solutions, they must present data and documentation of its efficacy. Donors are not looking for miracles; they are looking for answers. No, not guarantees, but well-researched, field tested, innovative solutions to problems confronting the people most at risk; particularly the poor, the elderly, and, most of all, children.

It's the grant-seeker's responsibility to convince those with ready financial assets that their approach to resolving a social, economic, environmental, or people problems is innovative, feasible, and ready to be fully implemented. Most of all, a proposal should offer the possibility of succeeding where others have failed, because trust me, many have failed and many have made similar overtures and promises. Success in the world of *Doing Good with Other People's Money* is not measured by how much funding is received, but more about what the money is used for and whether it made an impact, even in a small way. That is how success is measured and frankly, will determine whether your organization thrives or dives. Donors aren't cold-hearted. They have a legal responsibility to ensure that their assets are deployed in the most socially responsible manner possible, as defined by them, the funder, not by you, the asker.

GOVERNMENT AND FOUNDATION FUNDERS: SAME GOALS, DIFFERENT PROTOCOLS

While both government and foundation Donors have similar goals and expectations, they approach their missions differently. Government protocols, especially those at the federal level, are much more bureaucratic and rule-bound, making the processes both complex and cumbersome. I call it mind-bending. Government entities, whether at the local, state, or national levels, typically issue what are known as Requests for Proposals, or RFP's. Often taking years to prepare and issue, RFP's are typically loaded with details, arcane language, and must-do's requiring untold hours of response time.

FOUNDATION DONORS

Foundations, contrary to government funders, typically attempt to make life easier for submitters by initially requesting short-form responses, such as letter proposals or concept papers. This reduces the burden on submitters, donors, and reviewers. I call these screening proposals. This multi-step process works out quite well for all concerned. Foundations typically apply an "in-house ranking" or selection system known sometimes only to them. Those "above the line," based on a numeric score, are invited to submit full proposals, and those "below the line" are thanked for their efforts and politely dismissed from further competition. The above-the-liners are congratulated and then advised of the new submission dates and given new sets of instructions on how to submit the full proposal. This is done for consistency purposes so each proposal can be scored and ranked fairly on the same cost and deliverable criteria.

Typically, Donors and the nonprofits they fund respect their differing roles and purposes. Some Donors, like the classic mother-in-law, want to make their opinions known at every opportunity, while others allow the process to move forward without a heavy hand. Once the grant has been awarded, the ball is in the Doer's court, who must now prove they can do more than write a convincing proposal. It's time to turn words into actions. Put a different way, using sponsor speak, it would go something like this: "Based on binding contractual agreements, the Donor agrees to provide funding, in accordance with a prescribed schedule or achievement benchmarks and the Doer agrees to achieve the mutually endorsed results and outcomes and compliance with sponsor reporting and administrative requirements." And that's just part of it. Please keep in mind that Donors don't pay for learning, they pay for results.

While corporate donors follow a similar path as foundations, government donors are rule-bound, required to operate within highly structured environments with relatively little flexibility to go outside those pre-determined boundaries. Government agencies have the least amount of flexibility because their funding, operating missions, and priorities are defined for them by the executive and the legislative branches of government, with little room to maneuver due to bureaucratic and legal requirements.

Foundations, however, have more room to maneuver, depending on what type of foundation it is. They must remain cognizant of Internal Revenue Service rules and regulations they are required to follow. Their funding and operating priorities are defined by major donors, foundation leadership, and Boards of Directors. Grant seekers should always be sensitive to the diversity of missions and priorities out there, because when it comes to foundations, one size does not fit all.

TEN REASONS WHY NONPROFITS FAIL

- **Funding Priorities Have Changed**: Leaving the nonprofit adrift in search of a new mission and new funding sources because they neither diversified nor broadened their capabilities and interests or sought funding from alternative sources.

- **No Succession Plan:** The nonprofit is plodding along and prosecuting its mission as best they can, yielding little in the way of results. Leadership believes it's time to move on (a euphemism for closing its doors), sending the organization into a death spiral.

- **Diminishing Resources:** The nonprofit is experiencing a monetary dry spell and they are running out of operating capital. The only way they can survive is to downsize by shedding staff, merging with another non-profit, or closing their doors—guess what wins?

- **Competition/Survival of the Fittest:** there is an overabundance of similar nonprofits in the same geographical area competing for the same funds and for the same clients—some must die so others can live.

- **Mission Drift:** To remain relevant and recognized in their communities, some nonprofits take on programs and responsibilities outside their areas of expertise finding themselves unable to successfully prosecute their new assignment and the funder pulls its funding.

- **Big-Box Nonprofit Comes to Town:** A well-funded nonprofit with a national footprint comes to the neighborhood. Whether it's the YMCA, Habitat for Humanity, or the Red Cross, they become the "go-to" organization of choice. There's no way you can compete because they offer economies of scale and a huge support base that no local nonprofit can match. This is much like the devastation Walmart leaves in its wake as they move into a new town, forcing the mom-and-pop stores to close.

- **The Politics Have Changed:** The political party that supported your nonprofit organization and got you that start-up grant is no longer in power and your nonprofit finds itself on the outside looking in—what goes around comes around.

- **Internal Discord:** Leadership and board disputes have escalated with the Executive Director moving on to another nonprofit taking key personnel and with half the board members resigning, fatally damaging the organization's ability to successfully execute their mission. They have little chance for recovery.

- **Moving on to Other Causes:** Philanthropists like to spread the wealth around because they get recognition for doing those good deeds.

Perhaps major donors didn't like the direction the nonprofit was heading, or they just wanted to move on to another more popular cause.

- **Failure to Diversify**: Some nonprofits just fail to "read the tea leaves," believing their cause is a righteous one when the rest of the world has moved on. Remaining inflexible in a constantly changing world is an invitation to fail.

THERE'S ONLY SO MUCH MONEY TO GO AROUND

Bottom line: there is only so much money to go around, regardless of how noble the cause. There is an endless inventory of needs and wants, each as important to their champions as yours, but only a limited amount of funding. It doesn't mean your problem is not important or your solution unworthy of funding. It only means that funders either: (a) haven't fully recognized your organization's capacities, (b) have already committed their funding for the next several fiscal years, (c) have other interests or priorities, or, (d) there are more than enough problems to go around and not enough money to fund them all. Those are the realities facing organizations wanting to do good with other people's money. So before focusing on a problem to solve, make sure there is interest and money available to fund your "good deed doing."

WHAT IS FUNDED AND WHAT IS NOT?

Ultimately, the list of what social deprivation is "hot" and what is "not" or, what is fundable and what is not, is typically not within the grant seeker's control. However, that does not preclude grant seekers from doing some serious legwork. That is, familiarizing themselves with what types of nonprofits and causes different funders predictably support. They have their own mandates, preferences, and priorities. Be careful of those policy shifts that often occur, particularly with federal and state agencies. Political parties change places, and the "ins" become the "outs" and the "outs" become the "ins." When that happens, the power shifts, as do budget priorities. In the end, while it is possible to influence what nonprofit organizations get, such as directed funding, and what public-sector budgets contain, it is not typically within the political reach of most nonprofits. But it is within the reach of mega-nonprofits and of major research universities with the financial wherewithal to hire lobbyists to convince federal agencies and state officials to "line item" them into federal or state budgets.

At the end of the day, decisions are made as to what is funded and what is not, and sometimes rational minds prevail. Given the pantheon of problems, concerns, and inequities facing mankind and that mankind, in turn, perpetuates against our physical world and against each other, eventually decisions are reached as to what will be funded and what is not. Whether you agree with those decisions is of little concern to the Donor. That is my way of saying, "let it go if your nonprofit was left out in the cold." It may be time to move on and find different funding opportunities. It would not hurt to politely ask why the sponsor didn't fund you, because you'll want to know what you can do better the next time to earn their trust and money. Above all, do not challenge their decision. Accept this as a learning experience and move on—your turn may come later.

I DIDN'T SAY IT WAS GOING TO BE EASY

Pursuing and winning grants is complex and highly competitive. There will be detours and mental gymnastics, some shaking of collective heads as you dip your toes in the grant pool. As you get in deeper and deeper, you might start questioning your sanity (as well as your vocabulary) as you attempt to learn a new language I call "grantese." There will be some sleepless nights as proposal deadlines loom menacingly. Your self-esteem will be wounded by non-descriptive rejection letters, causing you to wonder, "What did we do wrong?" *It's the learning curve thing*, you think. You start questioning your commitment and capability, wondering why those grants and contracts are not rolling in.

Be rest assured, if your journey through the grant-getting maze is completed, and if you faithfully apply the principles and techniques outlined in this book, you will come out the other side with an enhanced ability to compete for, and ultimately win, grants and contracts. That will make the effort worthwhile not only for your organization, but more importantly, for the communities you will serve.

CHAPTER 5

Nonprofits to the Rescue

N onprofits, as a group, are at various times referred to as the Voluntary Sector, the Nonprofit Sector, the Third Sector, and Civil Society. No matter what they are called, their primary mission is to enrich society by focusing on the creation of "social wealth," rather than the creation of personal wealth. They come in all sizes, colors, and shapes, with the clear majority being small "mom and pop" operations. Then there are the mega-nonprofits with instantaneous name recognition; highly-tuned and successful grant- and contract-getting machines with ready access to the media and potential donors and with political clout at all government levels. They are the museums we visit, the hospitals that treat us, the colleges and universities that educate us, the public television stations that entertain and inform us, the surrogates who care for us, the big brothers and big sisters we, perhaps, never had. They are our conscience and internal guidance systems, they protect our planet for us, and above all, they remind us all that we are not alone and that others might need our help.

But what about all those small or not-so-small nonprofits who work in the shadows without receiving much public applause, support, or recognition? What about the ones who get energetic support from some, but are reviled by others? Big, small, or in-between, they have one thing in common: nonprofits need money to operate and to do what they do (with some needing more than others).

OVER EXTENDED AND UNDERFUNDED

A recent survey of the nonprofit sector by the Nonprofit Finance Fund (NFF), found that our nations' nonprofits are, to some degree or another, in financial distress for two primary reasons: First, government funding has not increased to meet the needs of existing nonprofits, and second, philanthropic dollars are harder to obtain, while, at the same time, the need for services has risen dramatically. Clearly, nonprofits need, according to the NFF, new funding sources and models. Nonprofits receiving government funding are facing particularly strong headwinds, with 83% of those receiving federal funding not being reimbursed for the full cost of services and most payments are late in coming. Some 25% of all nonprofits have less than thirty days of operating capital on hand. While this is happening, over 50% of the nonprofits say they cannot meet existing service demands. In response to these shortfalls, 39% plan to change the ways they raise and spend money, with an equal number having collaborated with sister nonprofits to improve or increase services while others are enhancing technology to improve organizational efficiency.[1]

GOVERNMENT TO THE RESCUE?

The federal government uses a variety of funding mechanisms to achieve national priorities through partnerships with nonprofit organizations that are directly involved in a wide range of missions, including health-care, education, poverty, community development, criminal justice, and other areas of social need. Federal agencies and nonprofits (along with for-profits) sometimes partner up, using their combined experience and social leverage to achieve high priority social goals.

Why do this? Because it promotes economic effectiveness and efficiency. In other words, local nonprofits have local knowledge,

---

1   www.nonprofitfinancefund.org/announcements/2013/state-of-the-non profit-sector-survey

physical proximity to those in need, available and trained workforce, and flexibility, and they can provide services at a lower cost to on-the ground situations as they evolve.

HOW FEDERAL FUNDS REACH NONPROFITS

- The most direct route is grants, cooperative agreements, and contracts. In turn, nonprofits provide support and services to targeted populations and beneficiaries. Grants are provided to nonprofit organizations under 700 different federally-funded programs.

- Federal grants and contracts find their way to nonprofits through intermediary organizations, including states, localities, housing authorities, regional governmental entities, school districts, and the like.

- Federal funds flow to nonprofit organizations as contracts and fees for service. While following a more complex route, they eventually end up where intended; that is, reimbursing nonprofit hospitals, nursing homes, hospice facilities, and other nonprofit health care providers for services provided to eligible recipients in the Medicaid or Medicare programs.

COMPETING FOR GOVERNMENT CONTRACTS: WHERE TO BEGIN

While contracts, on the surface, appear like grants, there are major differences, including: required deliverables, higher levels of risk to the bottom line, potential for sanctions and financial penalties, and more rigorous compliance and oversight. These differences must be fully considered before you even think about applying for a contract.

As with grant submissions, you want to start the process by working backwards from the required submission date, which is very unforgiving. You must also develop a writing plan that is not only consistent with that schedule, but will ensure the response is consistent with all funder/ contractor requirements. Contracts are replete with requirements, and even penalties, for non-performance.

Do not underestimate the complexity of this process. Make sure you have the time, the right assets, and manpower, as well as expertise and staff, if you are considering competing for contractual opportunities. It wouldn't hurt to have the telephone numbers of contract-savvy consultants who can guide your organization through the process. The first question you must ask yourself is whether you have the capacity to meet all current obligations without disrupting ongoing work flow, let alone taking on new responsibilities and whether you could operate a new venture within your existing organizational envelope. If the answer here is yes, you must explain how this new opportunity will be fully integrated into current operations and activities without causing either to be degraded.

TYPES OF CONTRACTS

All contracts and grants are governed by FAR, or Federal Acquisition Regulations, which establishes consistent policies and procedures for the acquisition of goods, products, and services. There are several different types of contractual vehicles. You will need to become conversant with them if you want to compete for contracts.

Types of government contracts include:

- **Fixed-Price:** If the contractor meets deliverables and spends less than the fixed price award, they get to keep the difference. If they spend more than the fixed price amount, they "eat it."

- **Cost Reimbursement**: This type of agreement minimizes contractor risk by receiving periodic reimbursement for funds expended. The downside to this is the administrative complexity, oversight, and reporting requirements that can become almost overwhelming.

- **Performance Contracts**: Here, the contractor gets financially reimbursed when the contractor achieves agreed-to contractual deliverables and outcomes, as defined in the executed agreement.

- **Task Order Contracts**: These types of contracts provide the greatest flexibility to government because they do not have to create new contractual vehicles every time a new contract is authorized—it's open-ended for an identified period.

- **Time and Materials:** These types of contracts are rarely, if ever, used for service type agreements since they are so open-ended and very difficult to measure.

WHAT CONTRACT SEEKERS NEED TO KNOW

Before even contemplating competing for a contract, you must understand that contracts are different than grants—very different. So please pay close attention to this chapter. There are questions every nonprofit would have to answer and decisions they need to make before applying for a federal, state, or locally-sourced contract. Be very honest when you evaluate your capabilities, assets, technologies, human resources, and delivery capacities to determine if your organization is "contract ready." The only ones you would be fooling are yourselves and, ultimately, your organization—particularly if you were awarded a contract and you could not successfully deliver. So please be very forthright in identifying both your strengths and weaknesses. You need to understand the magnitude of the differences between contracts and grants before deciding whether to compete for contracts.

Ultimately, it is better to delay and build capacity, both human and technological, before you enter this new marketplace. Consider bringing experienced and contract-savvy personnel and/or consultants on board who can help guide you through this process.

OPERATIONAL DIFFERENCES BETWEEN GRANTS AND CONTRACTS

We are going to get a bit more into the "weeds," because you need to fully understand the real difference between a grant and a contract and what it means for you, your organization, and your constituents.

GRANTS	CONTRACTS
The government uses grants to support and to stimulate an activity and to advance the public good	Contracts are used to procure a service or product for the direct benefit of government
Grants are awarded after a review of technical merit	Contracts are awarded based on overall "best value" which includes technical factors as well as price
Grants are not government cost-estimated	Contracts are independently government cost-estimated
Grants have no formal protest process	Contracts allow formal protests
Grants cannot be used for classified work	Contracts must be used for classified work
The grant oversight agency is the Office of Federal Financial Management	The contract oversight agency is the Office of Federal Procurement Policy
Grants require best efforts	Contracts require the delivery of promised goods or services
Grants allow for flexibility in defining the scope of work	Contracts have a rigid and defined scope of work
Grant non-performance may lead to a default	Contract non-performance is a default
Grants are easy to amend or revise	Contract modifications must meet strict standards
Grants are usually renewable	Contracts are usually not renewable
Grants are not typically held to a timetable	Contract milestones are strictly enforced
Grants allow for sub-awards	Contracts have limits on subcontracting
Grants are eligible for advance payments	Contract payments are based strictly on deliverables
Applicants define the grant scope of work	Government defines the scope of work for contracts
Grantees are encouraged to publish	Contractors require prior approval for publications
Key personnel on grants have flexibility to change time and effort	Contractors require prior approval to alter time and effort

REVIEWING CONTRACT RFP'S

If nonprofits decide not to compete for contracts, it may be dismissing an opportunity to enter a new marketplace and expand their portfolios and services. On the other hand, spending considerable time, effort, and money responding to funding opportunities that you don't really have the chops to win, like contracts, can also be costly. To help nonprofits decide whether any contract funding opportunity is within your wheelhouse, I am providing a decision support questionnaire to guide you.

CONTRACT ASSESSMENT QUESTIONNAIRE

Be scrupulously honest with your answers—otherwise you might find yourselves competing for an opportunity that is way above your current capabilities and, even worse, being awarded the contract and royally screwing things up by ultimately making your nonprofit ineligible for future funding opportunities.

1. Does the RFP describe activities and services that are both a good fit and compatible with your organization's current business model, expertise, capabilities, and interests?

Yes_____ No_____ Maybe _____

2. Is your organization financially stable?

Yes_____ No_____ Maybe _____

3. Does the RFP's funding formula cover all direct and indirect costs?

Yes_____ No_____ Maybe _____

4. Is this the type of service your community and current clients would benefit from and want?

Yes_____ No_____ Maybe _____

5. Do you currently possess the necessary facilities, staff expertise, knowledge, and technical competence to successfully achieve all the deliverables, outcomes, and requirements within the RFP established timetable?

Yes_____ No_____ Maybe _____

6. Is your organization willing to accept the risks inherent in competing for a new funding opportunity? That is, possibly not winning the award?

Yes_____ No_____ Maybe _____

7. Does your organization have sufficient financial reserves or "rainy day funds" to support you through what could be a very complex and demanding organizational transition?

Yes_____ No_____ Maybe _____

8. Can you maintain existing services while at the same time competing for and carrying out your new expanded obligations?

Yes_____ No_____ Maybe _____

9. Have you conducted a competitive analysis? And based on that analysis, does your nonprofit have at least a greater than 50% chance of being awarded the contractual opportunity?

Yes_____ No_____ Maybe _____

10. Have you identified potential "teaming partners" to enhance both your competitive positions?

Yes_____ No_____ Maybe _____

11. Are you confident that your cost proposal will be in the competitive range?

Yes_____ No_____ Maybe _____

12. Has your organization every competed for and been awarded a contract? If yes, did you meet all contractual requirements on time and within budget?

Yes_____ No_____ Maybe _____

SCORING
Yes= 10 points
Maybe= 5 points
No=0 points

CONTRACT ASSESSMENT QUESTIONNAIRE

INTERPRETING YOUR SCORES
95-120: Go for It!

Your organization is a fine-tuned machine. Perhaps you've become complacent and it's time to reinvent yourselves, tackling new, perhaps more intransigent social issues and social needs. Contracts present a new opportunity to up your game and become more relevant and to demonstrate that you can compete because you have a better idea. Don't underestimate the complexity of moving from grants to contracts—it will take some learning, but it's something perhaps that your organization is ready to do. Go for it!

60-90: Dealer's Choice

You're almost there—close but not close enough. If you are closer to the "60" score, ask yourselves what can be done in the short term to refine and recalibrate your operating model, making it contract-friendly. Think about bringing in a consultant to review your operating model and to determine if new technologies and management approaches could add value. Sometimes "good is not good enough," so you might consider getting to "great" before pursuing contractual opportunities.

Less than 55 Points: Don't Pass Go

If your score is less than 55 points, this presents an opportunity to identify areas of weakness, upgrade current operating processes, re-train staff, review organizational structure and leadership capabilities, and communicate with clients so you can give you feedback on your existing programs, giving you the chance to note what improvements you can make. You are not ready to compete for the more complex contract funding opportunities. Build capacity and pay attention to the little stuff that's going wrong, putting yourself in the place of your clients. It's time to re-energize your current program activities.

Good luck to you all!

FEDERAL CONTRACT PROPOSAL TEMPLATE

Government agencies evaluate contract proposals in terms of how well you can articulate your performance capabilities. There are typically two simultaneous review processes: (a) technical evaluation of proposals made by technical specialists without knowledge of the costs factors; and (b) final contract awards are made by contracting officers and cognizant staff who consider both technical quality and cost to determine which proposal offers the "best" value to the government.

FACTOR 1: TECHNICAL APPROACH-Articulate your plan and approach, including a full discussion of the nature and scope of the project. Make sure your technical approach reflects a clear understanding of the work statement. Identify the results that must be achieved to meet all the requirements set out in the solicitation. Are the responses clear and focused? Does the proposal respond to all the needs and requirements of the proposed project? Is the proposal technically responsive? Describe the incremental activities and actions as well as their timeframes. Explain why you selected this approach and what advantages it offers the clients and the funder in terms of cost, time, and effort.

FACTOR 2: PAST PERFORMANCE-Identify projects with similar scope and complexity that your organization successfully completed. What factors made it successful? If not initially successful, what did you do to turn it around? Has your organization ever been sanctioned or received a negative program review?

FACTOR 3: MANAGEMENT APPROACH-Does your management approach reflect a clear understanding of project deliverables, tasks, and outcomes? Identify how the project team will deliver required services and define how the project will be executed, monitored, and directed. Are deliverables and outcomes identified and achievable? Identify the unique capabilities you bring to the table and the specialized expertise and/or technology that others do not possess.

FACTOR 4: MANAGEMENT EXPERIENCE–Proposed Project Director and Key Staff should include resumes to document work and academic history demonstrating they have the credentials and work experience to successfully carry out the project. Does your organization have sufficient internal resources, financial reserves, and experienced personnel necessary to successfully achieve the desired project outcome? Do you have access to additional human assets, including consultants or new hires, should that be necessary? Have you considered collaborations with other effective nonprofits with experienced personnel in the areas of need? Include an organizational chart, identify senior project leadership and key personnel, and outline their qualifications, making sure to identify board structure and membership.

FACTOR 5: QUALITY CONTROL–What is your plan for quality control when it comes to project activities and performance? Have you identified processes, procedures, and metrics which are predictive and sensitive to project permutations? Demonstrate your commitment to Quality Assurance as a continuous process. Does your quality assurance system focus on client expectations and outcomes, and how? Do you possess the ability and technology to track multiple activities and processes? Do you have a continuous improvement plan?

FACTOR 6: COST FACTORS–Provide a detailed budget. You should include, but limit yourselves to considering labor rates and salaries by title, supplies, equipment, facilities utilities, cost of delivering services, travel and transportation, costs of new personnel, required new technology, indirect cost rates, all related client costs, and "other." Also include potential revenues from fees and other sources, including grants and donations.

HOW FEDERAL CONTRACTS ARE RANKED AND SELECTED

Two separate and distinct reviews are performed: (1) competitive review of submitted and qualified proposals, and (2) past performance assessment

Competitive Review

When dealing with contracts, proposals are evaluated individually, not against others. They are compared against the factors in the solicitation called the Performance Work Statement (PWS). Additional evaluative factors might be added depending on the specific solicitation. Proposals must include all required factors to be fully responsive. How well you articulate and document each factor will determine the score and whether the proposal will be funded or not.

Reviewers and raters identify strengths and deficiencies for each evaluation factor or sub-factor. The rating standards follow a risk level scale based on the evaluation panel's assessment as follows: Exceptional (E); Good (G); Acceptable (A); Marginal (M); and Unacceptable (U).[2]

Past Performance Review

Reviewers will consult the Past Performance Information Retrieval System (PPRIS) database to determine a submitting business' performance risk. The system aggregates contractor past performance data, allowing the federal acquisition community to make informed decisions. This is in addition to reviews of provided references.

A Risk Rating is then assigned:

• Unknown Risk/UR: No record of past performance

---

2   FDIC OMWI Education Module: Preparing Technical Proposals for Government Contracting

- Low Risk/LR: Consistently meets performance standards and contract terms without failure

- Moderate Risk/MR: Offeror meets work schedules, provides specified services and meets contract terms without failure

- High Risk/HR: Offeror has consistently not met work schedules and other obligations, has defaulted on at least one contract within the past three years, or has chronically failed to meet contract terms.

Reviewers and raters identify strengths, weaknesses, and deficiencies for each evaluation factor or sub-factor. The rating standards follow a "risk level scale" as well, and these are based on the evaluation panel's assessment: Exceptional (E); Good (G); Acceptable (A); Marginal (M); or Unacceptable (U).

Best Value Determination

Ultimately, it's the proposal that offers "the best value" that achieves the highest ratings. Best value is not just about price, but is a collaborative judgement made by experienced reviewers who consider other factors including capability, capacity, and past performance.

Clearly, contracts are more complex to manage and administer than grants and potentially more problematic because contractors can be held financially and legally responsible for non-compliance. The Federal Government, recognizing the complexity of contracts, the importance of competition, and particularly wanting to encourage small and minority owned businesses to compete for federal contracts and procurements, sponsors two national networks to assist any organization wanting to do business in the government space.

ASSISTANCE IS AVAILABLE
Small Business Development Centers

The U.S. Small Business Administration, together with states, fund some 900 Small Business Development Centers (SBDC's) across the U.S., providing a vast array of technical assistance to small organizations and aspiring entrepreneurs around the U.S. and Puerto Rico. Their focus is on creating new business owners and assisting existing small businesses to remain competitive in the complex marketplace of an ever-evolving global economy; to turn small businesses into big businesses. Services are free and centers offer face-to-face consulting in all areas related to small businesses and at-cost training on topics including: writing business plans, accessing capital, marketing, regulatory compliance, technology development, and international trade.

You can find your local Small Business Development Center by going to http://americassbdc.org/.home/find-your-sbdc/.

Procurement Technical Assistance Centers (PTAC)

PTAC is a nationwide network of procurement professionals working to help local businesses successfully compete in the government marketplace. Funded by the Defense Logistics Agency and with over three hundred local offices nationwide, their primary purpose is to assist local businesses successfully compete for federal contract and procurement opportunities. PTACs are the bridge between government and suppliers and contractors. You can locate PTAC offices and training opportunities by going to this website: http://www.aptac-us.org/contracting-assistance/ptac-training-events-/

WHY GOVERNMENT CONTRACTS WITH NONPROFIT ORGANIZATIONS

Governments at the federal, state, and local levels contract with nonprofits for two primary reasons. First, government lacks the knowledge, the facilities, the staff, the infrastructure, and the delivery capabilities that nonprofits have been developing and delivering for well over a hundred years. Second, if government were to get in to the business of providing comparable services, it would take years to build and ultimately cost more for perhaps less robust services than what is currently delivered by nonprofits.

CONTRACT OPPORTUNITY SEARCH ENGINES: FEDBIZOPPS

This searchable database lists all federal government contracting opportunities exceeding $25,000, including major solicitations, contract awards, subcontracting opportunities, and other procurement opportunities that are required to be posted. The U.S. Government is the largest single purchaser of goods and services in the world, awarding $500 billion in contracts every year. The U.S. Small Business Administration works with federal agencies to award at least 23% of all prime government contract dollars to small and disadvantaged businesses. I can tell you, from personal experience, that it's fairly easy to navigate the FedBizOpps search engine.

System for Award Management (SAM) (http://www.SAM.gov)

Please note that while both www.fedbizopps and www.grants.gov remain free standing, as of now, they will ultimately be integrated into the SAM system. SAM not only aggregates multiple systems, but is also expected to create a more streamlined user experience—which, from my perspective, is not ready for primetime yet. SAM is the federal government's new Award Management System and is anticipated to aggregate separate opportunity search engines, currently managed in separate locations by separate government entities, into one unified system.

Who Can Use SAM

SAM is available to any individual or organization interested in doing business with the Federal Government or wanting to know what funding opportunities are available to them including: vendors, grantees, contractors, nonprofits, for-profits, faith-based organizations, federal assistance recipients and those seeking assistance, public users searching for government business information, or anyone just curious about what our government is doing with their money.

Accessing the SAM System

Getting access to this new consolidated system requires you to register as a SAM user, even if you were registered in one of the legacy accounts previously. There is no fee for registration. However, the SAM site warns that if you get an email, text, or phone call from a company asking you to contact them right away about your SAM.gov registration, be cautious. These messages are not from the Federal Government. It's FREE TO REGISTER in SAM.gov for any individual or entity. You engage third party vendors at your own risk.

I have attempted to understand and to navigate SAM, and my experience was less than successful. This is not an intuitive system. Rather, while solving long-standing issues and concerns, new ones were created. There is more complexity for the user because of integration issues, the size of the new database, and unfamiliarity with the new integrated system when compared to the more intuitive grants.gov or FedBizOpps.gov systems. Navigation proved to be less intuitive than developers would have you believe. Because SAM includes information of various sensitivity levels, requiring "selective" access for some and not for others, it does add some new complications. Information and access is segregated based on "need to know" or "eligibility" and security clearances. Every new system, especially one as complex as this, goes through the teething stage. And please, take the warning about third party assistance very seriously.

CHAPTER 6

Creating a Lean, Green, Grant-Getting Machine

A big part of the learning curve is recognizing that success in any meaningful endeavor does not come easily. The first step is learning what it takes to create a lean, green, and sustainable grant- and contract-getting machine. This chapter will examine the Five Stepping Stones those wanting to do good with other people's money must both adopt and apply to be eligible for grant and contract funding from government, corporations, and foundations. It won't be easy, but is anything worthwhile ever easy?

STEPPING STONE #1: OBTAINING NONPROFIT STATUS: THE BASICS

Before you even think about doing good with other people's money, or writing a proposal, you must first have a passion, purpose, mission, or goal. And no, winning grants or contracts is not one of them, at least not yet. You must first build an organization that is eligible to compete for, receive, and financially account for sponsor funding. An organization capable of delivering a good or service that will make a community a better place. In other words, you are in the problem-solving business. If your organization is new to the game, then you have some ground to make up before you can even ask for funding from anyone.

First you must qualify for and be approved for 501(c)(3), or nonprofit status, by the Internal Revenue Service (IRS).

Applying for Nonprofit Status

Applying for nonprofit status can and will be a challenge, so don't expect it to happen quickly. Remember, you are dealing with the IRS. It will take time, patience, lots of paperwork, and money. In fact, you might want to seek assistance from professionals with experience in these matters, like a lawyer, an accountant, or a nonprofit that has already qualified and is willing to shepherd you through this somewhat byzantine process.

Qualifying for 501(c)(3) nonprofit status requires applicants to be organized as a corporation, trust, or unincorporated association with articles of incorporation, bylaws, and a stated mission or purpose which must further its exempt purposes. The most common types of 501(c)(3) organizations are charitable, educational, or religious in nature, and these are further defined in the tax code as to who they are and what they may do. Qualifying organizations are further classified by the IRS tax codes either as a public charity or a private foundation, with the primary difference being the source of financial support. Public charities have a broad base of support (many donors and contributors), while private foundations typically have only a few sources of financial support.

Before you even think about applying for a grant, you should always be aware of the obligations and restrictive covenants you must accept and be held accountable for when applying for nonprofit status: You cannot (a) participate in political campaigns, (b) lobby, (c) benefit any private shareholder or individuals, (d) operate for private interests, or (e) engage in illegal activities.

Federal tax law also imposes requirements and responsibilities on organizations granted nonprofit status, including: keeping accurate financial records, identifying sources of support, and describing programs and activities to ensure consistency with IRS nonprofit classifications. Nonprofits must annually submit information and financial returns as required and as specified by the IRS, including the documenting of charitable contributions and providing donors with written acknowledgement for contributions of $250 or more. Applying for nonprofit status requires the applicant to submit numerous forms and to make numerous disclosures. The IRS tax specialist reviewing your application can request additional information and put you at the bottom of the pile if you don't respond promptly or, unfortunately, if the political appointees don't view you as a "fellow traveler." Since it could literally take years to receive a final or even a favorable IRS ruling, patience is paramount. If, after all that time and all those forms, the IRS determines that your organization meets the requirements for exemption, they will issue a determination letter recognizing your newly-minted tax-exempt status. Bottom line, depending on the complexity and perhaps the politics of the submitting organization, the process will be frustrating, but it's a hurdle you must jump.

CONGRATULATIONS, YOU ARE NOW ELIGIBLE TO COMPETE FOR GRANTS

Once approved, you become eligible to apply for and receive government, foundation, and corporate grants. Additionally, donations or contributions made by individuals to your organization are now tax deductible. This is a critically important incentive for donors. You can substantially reduce the time, effort, and cost of obtaining nonprofit status by affiliating or merging with an existing IRS-approved 501(c)(3) nonprofit. It might be, especially for new nonprofits, an easier and less expensive route to start doing all those good things you've thought about for so long.

In addition to being recognized as a designated 501(c)(3) organization, nonprofits and the other usual suspects seeking and/or applying for federal funding must also register with both DUNS (Data Universal Numbering System) and SAM (System for Award Management). Registering with both DUNS and SAM is free for nonprofits. It sounds worse than it is, but you must register; that is, if you want access to all those federal funding opportunities (both grants and contracts).

STEPPING STONE #2: SURVIVING START-UP: SOME MAKE IT, MANY DON'T

Make no mistake about it: there are many obstacles remaining, even after obtaining your IRS-approved nonprofit status. Building an organization is one of them, and that takes money and personal commitment. The reality is that federal agencies don't provide start-up grants, nor do they typically give grants to unproven or untested organizations for any purpose. A Catch-22, wouldn't you say? So how do you get out of this box? You created the nonprofit for a reason—either there was a community-felt need, a problem that you believe is not being properly considered, or a personal reason why you established, a "paper" nonprofit.

HOW TO GET START-UP FUNDING

Many start-up nonprofits are funded by personal or private assets and/or donations from friends and associates, but rarely does that provide the necessary finances to operationalize your mission. Another alternative is to approach local political leaders, particularly state representatives, who can sometimes obtain what is called "member item funding" for back-home good deeds and for photo opportunities. The higher-up they are in the state legislative food chain, the more likely you are to get some much-needed seed funding. If that doesn't work, then think about your local unit of government, whether it is a town, municipality, or county. Many local governments receive block grant funding that passes through numerous hands and that can ultimately end up in yours, particularly, if you can show how you will contribute to the betterment of your local politician's career or add value to your community.

You can also make a "special pleading" for locally-sourced tax dollars if you can prove that enough voters are supportive of this endeavor.

Perhaps you can identify community or family foundations that provide grants to worthy causes if you are fortunate enough to have one that operates within your geographical area. Local foundations are particularly interested in homegrown initiatives. Alternatively, you can appeal to larger, well-funded nonprofits currently operating in your area and either seek their financial support or negotiate a services contract. One approach many colleges and universities capitalize on is inviting well-heeled members of the community to serve on Boards of Directors. Most know the rules of the game and, if accepted, the new board member typically understands they will eventually be asked to provide financial support or donations.

In fact, the National Council of Nonprofits reports that more than 75% of all charitable nonprofits have annual incomes of less than $25,000, and goes on to conclude that most of America's nonprofits are small community-based groups meeting primarily local needs. The Council estimates that up to 275,000 nonprofits, while maintaining their nonprofit status, are functionally defunct[1].

Many nonprofits are really nonprofits in name only, with very few becoming fully operational and able to prosecute their purported missions. Those that do are now in position to build an organization with staying power. And, the best way to do that is to invite local legislators, political and business leaders, and community members to join your board. Sustainable funding streams are critical to long-term success. Otherwise, you will be pleading for money outside your local Walmart. It's the nonprofit equivalent of survival of the fittest.

STEPPING STONE #3: INFRASTRUCTURE, CAPABILITY, GROWTH AND MISSION

Those receiving their 501(c)(3) are not yet free and clear of all those "possible horribles" that can inflict new organizations. Particularly

---

1   www.nonprofit.about.com/b/2011/06/09/the-irs-ax-finally-falls-on-nonfil-ing-nonprofits.html

those taking their eyes off their primary purpose by constantly shifting mission to follow the dollars or the problem of the day. If that describes your organization, it's time to perhaps rethink your future direction. Unfortunately, new and smaller nonprofits are at a disadvantage when it comes to winning contracts for a host of reasons, including: (a) they have yet to build a track record and prove themselves; (b) they lack the requisite administrative and financial infrastructure to operate and administer grants or contracts; and (c) they do not possess the knowledge, experience, personnel, or capacity to successfully compete for grants or contracts without obtaining significant start-up funding[2].

STEPPING STONE #4: THINK BIG, START SMALL

Recognizing that successful nonprofits require more than fees for services or personal donations to grow their enterprise, it is now time to seek other more predictable and sustainable funding sources. In this case, a mix of grants and contracts. There are several alternative approaches to acquiring grant and contract expertise and capability: (a) build internal expertise and learn the ins, and outs and the new responsibilities that both grants and contracts would impose on the organization; (b) redirecting, retraining, and refocusing existing personnel to become more grant- and contract-centric by becoming more knowledgeable about grants and contracts; (c) hiring proven and tested grant- and contract-savvy employees, if you have the financial wherewithal; (d) partnering with nonprofits that have proven grant- and contract-getting experience; or, (e) hiring consultants who have been there and done that.

STEPPING STONE #5: CHANGE, ADAPT OR BECOME IRRELEVANT

It's now time to step back, be thankful for your successes, congratulate yourselves for your good work, and prepare for the next operational

---

2   www.urban.org/uploadedPDF/412674

stage: locking in your gains. The future has a way of sneaking up on us; we must be prepared. Every organization, be it public, private, nonprofit, religious, or educational, needs a vision. We can create that vision or let circumstances determine our vision. My preference is to create our future vision rather than playing a constant guessing game. That is called your "Strategic Enterprise Model."

Grant- or contract-getting doesn't happen on its own; you make it happen. You do this by realigning your mission, capabilities, and operational capacities with the interests, funding priorities, needs and expectations of donors; government, foundations, and corporations. Your business model, your organizational structure, and the technologies and human assets that served you well in previous years might not match up with the constantly-changing priorities of donors, clients, volunteers, or constituents. In this rapidly-changing world, both grant- and contract-seekers and Doers must remain agile and prepared to respond to changing funding priorities and opportunities. Always keep in mind, "first in, first to win." Remaining flexible and taking an organic approach to achieving financial goals is what will let you survive the changes in political administrations and the inevitable re-prioritizing of what is important and what is not, what needs to be funded and what does not, and the rapidity of technological innovation. Above all, stay focused and true to your constituencies, your mission, and your communities.

STAY AHEAD OF THE FUNDING CURVE

Becoming a player with staying power requires your organization to be fully proficient at winning grants and contracts. The best way is to ease yourselves into the process by walking before running; that is, first applying for smaller grants or contracts, those too small for the "big dogs," or by becoming a sub-grantee to a larger nonprofit. Then, slowly and methodically build your delivery and administrative capacities and your understanding of this new world you have chosen to enter. With each success or collaboration, you will have gained experience and a track record, putting you on course for bigger and more complex opportunities. As your organization matures, and as the tasks, programs, and projects grow in scope and complexity, their consequent administrative and financial requirements become more complex as well. Staying ahead of the curve—that is, looking forward, not backward—is your best long-term growth and survival strategy. I always say there are good problems and bad problems, and being successful and requiring an organization to "scale up" is one of those good problems. Do this before the workload gets out of hand and you can longer balance the new demands with existing obligations and activities.

You will now have to create both a project and an administrative infrastructure to manage your awards. You can do this by moving some of your more experienced project personnel into these newly-created developmental, operational, and supervisory positions. However, doing this could strip out the infrastructure that kept those programs working and effective. Or, you can seek experienced new personnel if you have the financial capacity.

Once establishing a record of success with funders, you will find your grant and contract conversion, or success rate, going higher and higher and the need for additional program, administrative and financial capability and expertise becoming ever more important. Ultimately, economies of scale will reduce overhead costs and potentially generate a sustainable income stream for your organization. Provided, of course, you remain laser-focused on outcomes and the sponsor is kept satisfied, supportive of your efforts, and always in the loop. You can do this by continually assessing progress, self-correcting deviations from goals and objectives before they get out of hand, and ultimately, by doing what the proposal said you would do.

WHY SOME SUCCEED WHEN OTHERS FAIL: REDUX

So, let's get back to my original premise, why some succeed when others fail. We are always making comparisons or always wondering why some organizations and people succeed where others fail, even if the problems, the circumstances, the complexities, and the desired outcomes were all the same.

Humans make up the most complex social systems on earth. We have preferences and patterned behaviors that either contribute to our abilities and willingness to navigate this world or not. We respond to different situations and inputs with different degrees of acuity and effectiveness, and when faced with adversity some flee, others quickly raise their hands in surrender, yet others never give up until they have been defeated. So, what differentiates successful grant and contract getting organizations from those languishing in the proverbial pit of despair?

Behaviors of Highly Effective Grant- and Contract-Winning Organizations

- They accept complexity and uncertainty as everyday realities.

- They recognize that success and reputation are built on a foundation of responsiveness and accomplishment to funders and clients.

- They say what they will do, and then do what they say–always.

- They recognize that the devil is in the detail and that writing successful proposals is all about detail.

- They actively engage community residents and institutions in program and proposal development.

- They remain grounded in their primary mission.

- They stick to what they know and do best.

- They remain collaborative and open, willing to share expertise and knowledge with others.

- They seek partnership opportunities when it's in the best interest of the nonprofit, constituents, and collaborating organizations.

- They strive for excellence in all situations and endeavors, but maintain realistic expectations about what can be done when confronting hard problems and challenges.

- They are willing to accept and learn from failures rather than repeat those experiences.

- They stay agile, always ready and willing to face the next challenge with energy and confidence.

- They're quick on their feet and able to rapidly recognize and shift priorities and resources to meet new challenges without drama or angst.

- They hold themselves accountable.

- They involve themselves only in opportunities that are within their reach and capabilities.

- They can separate what is worthwhile to pursue and what is not.

- They would rather turn down an award that is not a "good fit" than deliver a substandard outcome.

- They think strategically, not organically. Organic thinkers allow events to just randomly evolve, while strategic thinkers analyze and rationally explore options selecting the most appropriate pathways forward.

- They seek sustainable growth, not one-time victories or explosive growth which cannot be sustained in the long-run.

Do you see yourself in any of these statements? Would you want to work for this type of organization with these values and qualities? Could this be a model for you or your organization to follow and replicate? Think about it. Think hard about it, because that's what it takes to build successful grant- and contract-getting organizations.

CHAPTER 7

You Gotta Have a Plan

W hether you are an existing nonprofit facing headwinds or just a general failure to thrive, there is hope and a way forward. Success in any nonprofit—or for-profit business venture, for that matter—requires an articulated vision, mission and purpose, a can-do attitude, a focus on what you do and how you do it, financial, intellectual, technological, and human resources and infrastructure, and a unique idea.

Your mission must have traction within the community and be recognized as innovative and responsive to a felt need by power brokers and opinion leaders, which is ultimately manifested through public recognition, donations, grants, contracts, and volunteerism.

As I previously said, without a plan and a strategic enterprise model, it's not whether your nonprofit will falter or fail, but when! *In fact, 8 out of 10 nonprofits close their doors within 18 months of opening them.* And they typically fail for the same reasons as their for-profit counterparts, which are: (1) not being in touch with community or with what they really need or want; (2) failure to differentiate themselves from the rest of the herd; (3) unable to articulate a need or mission that resonates with the community; (4) have yet to craft a unique selling proposition; (5) lacking financial expertise and the ability to formulate a viable income-generating business model; (5) turning a "blind eye" to competitive forces; and (6) overestimating the willingness of others to support their cause. By then, it's too late to turn the ship around and the money runs out.

So, why does this happen? Lots of reasons, but one fatal flaw always stands out: believing your own inner voice and assuming you know what is needed and what is best without checking your "inner reality" with the actual realities of the community you're looking to serve. In other words, someone didn't do their homework. It's one thing to have confidence in yourself, it's another to jump into unfamiliar waters before checking for crocodiles. The crocodiles will surely cheer you on, as will the competition because they know something you don't—they know the *marketplace* and they have a PLAN!

DONORS DON'T PAY FOR LEARNING, THEY PAY FOR RESULTS

Let me tell you what the grant-getting plan is not: it's not a disconnected set of random "coulda, woulda, shoulda's." Rather, it's a replicable sequence of purposeful and integrated actions and activities designed to achieve a desired result that is responsive to environmental inputs (also known as "life happens"). So, what does this jargon mean? It means that if you don't have a well-defined viable business model, you will fail. Your business plan and how well it aligns with the needs and wants of the community determines whether you will be at the head of the line or the back.

Always remember, you are representing the interests of those who cannot advocate for themselves, the ones left on the side of road. It's your obligation to fight for them. Your failure becomes their failure, and you don't want that to happen. If you want to add value to the lives of others, those who have yet to successfully navigate life's gives and takes, then you must both fully comprehend and affirmatively represent their interests by identifying causes and then implementing solutions, either individually or through social innovations. Solutions don't happen in a vacuum; it takes resources, staff, and money, and grant-getting is one of the best ways to make those good things happen.

DON'T OVERREACH

It becomes painfully obvious to Donors when you're just blowing smoke or when your claims ring hollow, since you're in start-up mode with nary a dollar in the bank or a success under your belt. That type of over-heated rhetoric and chest-thumping in a proposal smacks of desperation and creates un-realizable expectations. When this happens, you're only fooling yourself, because you will start believing your own hype and the sponsor will quickly conclude you are a bunch of desperate amateurs willing to say and do anything to get that grant. If you even hope to turn donors into supporters, you must earn their respect by proving you can deliver a service or program professionally, on time, and within budget, by focusing your energies, efforts, and capabilities on what you do well, not what you hope to do well in the future.

CONSIDER ALTERNATE FUNDING MODELS

While grants and contracts are the primary sources of funding for many nonprofits, there are, indeed, other funding sources, including fees for service. Not every nonprofit views grant-getting as a necessary part of their funding mix (or worthwhile) because they are pursuing different business or funding models. Many nonprofits focus on grants or are paid to provide contractual services on behalf of local, state, or federal entities. Some nonprofits receive their primary support from funding aggregators like United Way-type organizations, while others have a "fee for service" funding model, like the YMCA. Yet others focus their funding energies on individual giving, while some hedge their bets by deploying a diversity of funding approaches to mitigate risk and to smooth out funding cycles. One path is not necessarily better than the other. Even if a nonprofit has other secure sources of funding, it might be worthwhile to investigate and consider alternate sources, such as grants and contracts, to enhance and diversify funding streams so as not to be dependent on a single source.

One of the most mission-critical decisions nonprofits need to consider is deciding whether grant- and contract-getting should even be part of their funding mix and how big a role they should play, if any. Pursuing grants and or contracts would most likely require changes to current business models, requiring new investments in infrastructure and administrative and financial capacities, as well as program and project management and bringing in new skill sets and a different mix of human and financial resources. Things are going to be different, but hopefully in a good way.

DOES YOUR ORGANIZATION HAVE A GRANT-CENTRIC ENTERPRISE STRATEGY?

Pursuing grants or contracts should never be an afterthought. The process should be firmly imbedded into the ethos and missions of the organization; it fundamentally changes the relationship between the organization and the individuals they serve. Donors typically think of you as their "client" or as their "delivery vehicle," responsible for providing an agreed-to service or product. You are representing the funder and acting on their behalf and as such, you are expected to accomplish what was promised.

There are always gives and takes. Pursuing grants and contracts as a primary funding mechanism does have some downsides. Understand that your range of operating freedom is limited to what is written in that grant or contract agreement. On the other hand, you have a consistent source of funding and a set mission and purpose.

So, what's your pleasure? Are you willing to change your enterprise model? That's what it might take to succeed in the grant- and contract-getting business. Are you willing to trade operational freedom for some degree of financial security? It's your decision, but a decision that must be jointly made and accepted by the governing board, leadership, and staff if it has even the hope of being successfully prosecuted. What about the clients you previously serviced and assisted? Can you maintain your existing client and financial base while refocusing your business and operating model to conform to local, state, federal, and private funder requirements? The answer: don't give up your "day job" until you are totally confident your organization can create a sustainable flow of funds.

IS YOUR ORGANIZATION OPERATIONALLY AND FINANCIALLY STABLE?

Donors don't want to award funds to financially unstable organizations. That is not a confidence-boosting scenario for any potential funder. Indeed, they might want letters of support from local government agencies, other funders, political and community leaders, even clients vouching for your "good-deed doing." They may even want to make unannounced visits to view facilities and talk with staff and clients. The reality is that you must first prove your capability and organizational competence; that means having a fully-functioning organization with roots in the community, a track record of accomplishment, and secure sources of funding. The sponsor wants to be assured that you have the chops to turn your words into actual deeds and that you can do what you said you were going to do before the money transfers from their hands to yours.

DO YOU HAVE A UNIQUE SELLING PROPOSITION?

If you are a startup with limited name recognition and real-world experience, you're facing an uphill funding battle on many fronts. That is why you need a unique selling proposition, which is a fancy way of saying you must differentiate yourself from those "other nonprofits" who provide the same types of services in the same area, aimed at a similar demographic. Think hard about this one: what separates you from the competition and why would a donor want to fund you? Why would a potential client want to go to you for services when they have other options available to them?

You are the untried and untested "newbie." You need to give them a reason and it better be a darned good one if you expect your funders and potential clients to change their loyalties. Fail to do this and you will become just another statistic; another dropout on the road to doing good with other people's money. I can't do it for you, because I don't know what it is you want to do and if it's even worthwhile given the parade of nonprofits out there that have already been there and done that. So, what differentiates you from those others? If you can't make a very convincing case, I suggest you save your money and all the effort and angst that will surely come as you "flip" and "flop" about hoping to win a grant or contract.

DO YOU HAVE A BETTER IDEA?

Let me give you a hint—you, perhaps, have a better idea or a new technology that will excite the "money givers" and will solve all those problems that have been unassailable up until now. Do you believe you have a better way of working with the homeless or the drug addicted? Prove it with real hard data, and donors will beat a path to your door. Talk is cheap and you won't be given a chance to prove the value of your solution without having proof of concept. Make sure you have documentation that your idea works and indeed offers higher probabilities of success than those currently in the marketplace. Before you even contemplate entering a new market or service arena, make sure you perform a Competitive Analysis Scan to determine if there is a need for your services or if other organizations are already providing similar services.

DO YOU HAVE PRICING STRATEGIES?

Costing-out proposals is a complex task involving several competing demands and long-term considerations. Proposal writers and budget builders, typically two separate and distinct areas of expertise, must be in sync. That is, the "real" costs must be known to develop a coherent work plan. The budget is further complicated by the need to project costs into the future, because some grant and contract opportunities are for multiple years. Furthermore, there is a strategic push and pull between those that believe their chances are enhanced by being the low bidder and those believing the sponsor is not sensitive to costs but more concerned with bidder reputation and results. Sponsors are sensitive to price because they have already determined what the budget ranges should be for any announced funding opportunity. The low bidder, should they be awarded the grant or contract, can be penalized if they run out of funding before the project period ends and before all contracted outcomes are achieved. If that happens, the sponsor can require the awardee to make up the cost difference and complete the program as contractually agreed, or the program can be deemed noncompliant and the award terminated.

The opposite of underbidding, or low-balling, is referred to as budget stuffing, which is purposely over-estimating real costs to justify annual up-charges. Such obvious attempts are readily identified by the budget hawks, and they will not be favorably predisposed to funding organizations that have over-estimated actual costs. Those new to the grant and contract arena should be scrupulously honest when building the budget. However, a little underbidding might not hurt because it's more important to win that first grant, prove you can deliver on time and within cost, and deliver a credible product then to attempt to make a financial windfall your first time out of the gate.

DO YOU HAVE ALTERNATIVE DEVELOPMENT STRATEGIES?

Never become entirely dependent on one source of funding to finance your good deed doing. Nonprofits, faith based organizations, and schools must be prepared to invest in themselves, and some do. Capability does not spring forth from nothingness. Black holes, while interesting to contemplate, have no place in the world of grant- and contract-getting. People are not natural-born grant writers—they must be trained and succored, developed and valued. They are wordsmiths representing your organization and its mission, capabilities, and opportunities. They smooth out those rough edges, find the missing pieces of the puzzle, and establish trust relationships with donors because they "say what they will do and do what they say." If you say you have a capability and then are unable to deliver on that promise, the sponsor would have every right to pull that award, which, quite frankly, rarely happens. But they have long memories, so you wouldn't expect money from that sponsor again or any other within their circle, because they will make their experiences (both good and bad) known to others. Bottom line: it takes money to make money—and if you won't invest in yourselves, why would anyone else want to invest in you?

Sometimes it's better to collaborate than compete. Donors like, and oftentimes reward, partnerships, especially when each party brings something significant and new to the table. This could help both organizations reach new clients by providing a wider range of services and even expand the operations into other communities with similar needs for your now-combined services.

Ultimately, how well the proposal accurately represents your organization, its ideas and approach to solving problems, how well it reads, how well its ideas are formed, how well its logic flows, and how well it is presented, is all entirely within your control. I have seen too many shoddily-prepared proposals go out the door, only to leave a bad impression that is hard to live down. The proposal not only represents who you are and what you do, it determines whether you will be funded or not. Articulate, well-designed, and fully responsive proposals are more successful than shoddy last-minute submissions. You can come up with a whole bucketful of excuses as to why the proposal was not funded, but excuses don't keep the lights on—they're just sops to explain away why you weren't fully prepared to respond to the funding opportunity.

I have withdrawn proposals rather than submit a less than worthy product. Amateurish proposals with numerous typos and spelling and grammatical errors do not leave reviewers with a positive impression— shoddy proposal, shoddy work ethic.

COMPETITIVE ANALYSIS SCAN

Before deciding whether to enter the "grant- and contract-getting marketplace" it's critically important to focus on what you have to offer! That is, what separates you from the competition, or what can you do better, cheaper, or faster than the competition? Do you have a unique capability no other competing organization possesses or is capable of delivering? Before you commit to anything, regardless of how important and innovative you believe it to be, do what the private sector would do before entering a new marketplace: perform a competitive analysis to determine the likelihood of success before staffing, renting or expanding facilities, etc. It's often referred to as SWOT (Strengths, Weaknesses, Opportunities and Threats).

WHAT'S YOUR SWOT?

- Who else is out there sharing the same space, providing similar types of services, and working with the same clients? Name them.

- What are the key strengths of competitors and what do they do better than you?

- What do you believe you can do better than your competitors?

- Are the pricing models comparative? Can you reduce the unit cost of services to the sponsor?

- Have you heard complaints from the competition's clients about the services and assistance being provided?

- Are your clients satisfied with provided services?

- How do you intend on capitalizing on competitor weaknesses and replace them in both the marketplace of ideas and in the marketplace itself?

- Do you see opportunities for partnering with the competition?

- In what areas does your competition add value?

- In what operational categories can you add value to your competitors?

- In what functional categories can you compete successfully against your competitors?

IS YOUR NONPROFIT GROWING OR SHRINKING?

- Is the competition growing or shrinking their client or customer base?

- Are you growing or shrinking your client or customer base?

- How do you intend on growing your client base, given the presence or lack of direct competition? How do you plan on reaching out to existing and future customers or clients? What are their demographic characteristics?

- Do current clients value your services? Have you done satisfaction surveys? Do the competition's clients value their services?

- Are your clients required to participate in mandated services such as drug counseling or child abuse counselling and interventions? Or, can they select a provider of choice? Are your competition's clients required to participate in mandated services?

- Are there language issues, and does your staff have the capability to communicate with those who have limited English skills?

MARKETING AND OPPORTUNITY ASSESSMENT

- What strategies do you use to reach out to current and future clients?

- What strategies does your competition use?

- Is the competition's outreach more professional and "dialed in" to the community, power brokers, and clients?

- Are your current marketing strategies working for you? Why or why not?

- Are you actively deploying social media to stay in contact with your customer base? Is your competition more sophisticated in their deployment of technology than your organization currently is?

- Do customers and clients visit their respective online site?

- Does your organization have a consistent media presence? Does your competition have one?

- Does your staff attend community events and celebrations, offering information about your services and providing promotional items?

- Do you track the success of your promotional events and advertising?

- Are you having difficulty meeting your donor-promised deliverables and outcomes because you clearly overestimated either the need for your service or your abilities to attract clients? Is the competition experiencing the same shortfalls, or are they delivering on time?

- Do you give your clients opportunities to provide feedback? Does your competition?

WHAT'S THE CURRENT POLITICAL ENVIRONMENT?

- Are current government priorities at the national, state, and local levels financially and programmatically supportive of the types of services you are providing, and do they find them valuable?

- Are government regulations and requirements helping or restricting opportunities and efforts? If so, what can you do about it?

- Are there upcoming critical elections that can change or shift funding priorities that would have either a beneficial or detrimental impact on your organization and its current and future clients?

- Do you have people, colleagues, friends, or lobbyists representing your interests in the halls of government? Have they been successful, or are their pleas falling on deaf ears?

- Is your organization directly tied to one political party or another? Do you see that as an opportunity or as a threat?

WHAT'S THE CURRENT ECONOMIC ENVIRONMENT?

- Is the local, state, or national economy in distress?

- Is government attempting to jump-start the economy by moving money quickly into the public sector and to organizations equipped to help those in financial distress?

- Are the unemployed looking for new job opportunities, or are they seeking new job paths through retraining? Is government increasing funding for job training and job placement services?

- Are local and state governments cutting back on supporting nonprofits with block grant funding, or are they planning to increase funding?

- Who are your allies and how can you join in common cause to impact your collective funding futures?

WHAT'S THE CURRENT DONOR ENVIRONMENT?

- Are donors cutting back on funding?

- Are donors re-prioritizing as funding availability shrinks?

- Do donors go outside their comfort zones to fund new initiatives?

- What funding shifts and changes do you see occurring in the near and far term?

- Are there new opportunities for your organization as priorities change, or is the pie shrinking?

- What can you do to catch the next wave of funding?

- Are you attempting to diversify your funding mix to become less dependent on one donor or one type of donor?

- Are you interested in stepping into the government or foundation pond, or are you already there?

- Are you able to expand and diversify your services to attract a wider range of funding opportunities?

- Do you have name recognition with funders? Do you have a reputation for delivering high-quality services and meeting client needs? Are funders willing to discuss new funding opportunities with you?

CHAPTER 8

Getting From the "Why" to the "How"

U ntil now, I have been focusing on the "why" of grant and contract getting and why grants and contracts are critical funding sources for any organization believing they can do good with other people's money." The reasons nonprofits want to do good with other people's money are as diverse as there are sources of money to fund them and as varied as the demands people place upon them.

GRANTS AND CONTRACTS: CRITICAL TO NONPROFIT FINANCIAL SUSTAINABILITY

There are four primary reasons why nonprofits should become grant and contract savvy. First, it makes it possible for the nonprofit to fund their good deed doing and realize their varied missions. Second, winning grants and contracts contributes to financial sustainability, and without it, the prospects of survival are diminished. Third, you need a secure stream of income to hire and retain qualified staff. And lastly, reputation is sometimes worth more than money and your reputation for doing good work will bring you both recognition and additional funding opportunities.

SUCCESS DOESN'T JUST HAPPEN, YOU MAKE IT HAPPEN!

The road to becoming successful grant- and contract-getters, while not easy nor without detours, is probably one of life's most satisfying pursuits, because it is not about helping ourselves but about helping others. On this part of our journey, you will learn to walk the walk, talk the talk, and come out the other side fully equipped to win grants and contracts. Whether you are new to the world of Doing Good with Other People's Money and have a better idea requiring some seed funding, a small nonprofit surviving on local donations and the goodwill and sweat equity of volunteers and neighbors, or a school district that has too long relied on local taxes and state aid for funding, winning grants and contracts is in your future—or certainly should be.

Winning awards (grants and contracts) doesn't just happen on its own. You can plant the seed, but you still must harvest the crop; otherwise it will wither in the field. You cannot organically grow grants or contracts; you must strategically and methodically turn your ideas, your good deeds, and your hopes for others into a reality that donors understand and want to adopt as one of their funding priorities. Newly-organized nonprofits are advantaged in some ways, but not others. First, they haven't learned bad grant- and contract-getting habits or failed and fled after the first "no" or bailed out midstream because they didn't have a clue how to compete in the marketplace.

The newbies have an opportunity to start with a blank page and to create their grant- and contract-getting business model from the ground up. This is your nonprofit's opportunity to realign your business and enterprise models to more closely mirror and foster those new initiatives you've considered and reconsidered for so many years. This is one of the most significant decisions in the life of a nonprofit—the opportunity to remake themselves and to re-energize their employees and supporters (and most of all, to achieve financial sustainability).

THINGS CHANGE—SOMETIMES FOR THE BETTER, OTHER TIMES NOT

Your organizational structure, your mission and focus, your mix of human and technological assets, your funding model, and the needs of the community you serve may no longer be relevant as the world changes around you or as funding priorities shift. Many nonprofits find themselves either behind or too far ahead of the new funding curve. People's needs and problems are always evolving; some become more important and others less-so based on real and perceived values, beliefs, expectations, and policies of political leaders. Sometimes global warming tops the list of the most wanted, other times it could be global cooling, depending on your perspective. Sometimes green energy is our future, and other times it is natural gas. Other times it's about hunger or about abundance and what we do with it. Remember, I warned you about chasing the money and the same goes for chasing problems and the funding darling or priority du jour. But if there is one certainty in life, it's change. While staying focused on current tasks and opportunities, remain vigilant and sufficiently agile to follow that bouncing ball we call policy, because money always follows policy. Don't forget that your competition might have similar thoughts and interests in seeking new sources of funding and remember, "first in, first to win."

EVERY ORGANIZATION NEEDS A STRATEGIC ENTERPRISE STRATEGY

A Strategic Enterprise Strategy is a fancy way of saying a "business plan," and that applies whether you are a for-profit or nonprofit organization. Strategic models need to be modified and re-optimized when the world changes, people's needs and interests change, and funding priorities change. Doing things differently, entering new markets, facing new challenges, and attracting other people's money requires, I dare say, a new approach and a new business concept, also known as a new strategic enterprise strategy.

Confronting new market opportunities and their consequent "go forward" strategies can be more than difficult; it can, at times, be gut-wrenching. We question our own judgment for fear of destroying the organization we worked so hard to build. Perhaps the old operating model is no longer working and change becomes our only choice, but what change and how much? Perhaps you got too comfortable in your own niche and had no competition until now. Moving forward will place you in direct competition with your counterparts already imbedded in this new field. You know, the ones that are always at the head of the line when grant money is being sprinkled about. Change is scary, but so is not being invited to the party.

Melodramatic? Maybe, but sadly true. Don't fret, there is hope and a path forward to a new way of doing business.

THE WORLD CHANGES

As the world changes around us, we must be prepared to change with it. There are as many reasons why organizations want to get into the grant and contract getting businesses as there are stars in the sky (meaning the reasons are almost infinite). But what isn't infinite are grant- and contract-givers and their money. Whether new to the grant- or contract-getting world with a better idea requiring some seed money, a small nonprofit that has been surviving on local donations and the goodwill and sweat equity of volunteers and neighbors, or a school district that has relied too long on local taxes and state and federal aid for its annual funding, realigning your current enterprise model with your new business goals, strategies, and operational realities is the first step in the process.

LEAN FORWARD

What you used to do and how you did it might not adequately prepare your organization for what you need or must do now. That is, to become competitive grant- and contract-getters. Making your new strategic direction happen requires new thinking; redefining who you are and what you do, turning new ideas and business opportunities into operational realities that funders want to support. Your strategic enterprise model is your way forward. The first reaction to anything unfamiliar is discomfort, and even some fear, because we are comfortable with what we know, and oftentimes many will hold firm to those outdated ideologies until reaching the cliff's edge in defense of what was, and not of what can be.

DON'T BE A ONE-TRICK PONY

Nonprofits are not immune from competition; it's just a fact of life requiring considerable organizational energy and assets. We can never rest on our laurels; we must continually reinvent ourselves and our organizations, re-establishing our competitive position in our chosen fields of endeavor. That is, to put a stake in the ground signifying that you are now, and will always be, in the business of doing good with other people's money. Accomplishing this requires careful development, selection, and implementation of a "market basket" of new policies, tactics, approaches, and strategies that will advance both your cause and your competitive position with donors and the people you serve. Dependence on a single strategy, a single donor, a single capability, or a single delivery model is like being a one-trick pony. When that trick no longer brings in audiences, you're toast. Likewise, betting your future on a single strategy will not cut it in a world that values multi-capable, multi-functional, highly agile organizations. That is why several fully-integrated strategies need to be bundled into what is commonly referred to as the strategic mix. It is, in fact, this grouping and sequencing of strategies and consequent actions that ultimately determine how successful you are in capturing market position—or, in our world, other people's money.

The development, selection, implementation, and timing of new strategic initiatives involves thoughtful planning and analysis. Always take the "what if" approach before letting the new strategy run loose with potentially disastrous effect. The selected strategies should not only foster new enterprise goals and objectives, but should be consistent and supportive of organizational mission and purpose. Unless, of course, you want to change that, as well. New enterprise strategies should not be imposed, but rather integrated into current operations, allowing the new and the old to co-exist until a planned natural and nondestructive transition can take place. We are looking for better ways of doing things, not better ways of bringing the proverbial house down around our clients.

Having said that, no enterprise can long survive, let alone thrive, by thrashing about aimlessly or by trusting its future to luck or fate. Decisions made today determine success or failure tomorrow. Improperly-vetted strategies will just as surely lead to failure as having no strategic direction at all.

SELECTING YOUR BEST-FIT ENTERPRISE STRATEGIES

Never underestimate the importance of an Enterprise Strategy, because not having one would be equivalent to wandering the desert without a map. The Enterprise Strategy is your map to your organization's Promised Land.

I am providing nine model Enterprise Strategies for nonprofits, faith-based organizations, and schools, colleges, and universities wanting to: (1) enter the competitive grant or contract marketplace; (2) get a bigger piece of the pie by creating a dominant position in the marketplace; and (3) remaining viable, agile, and competitive in the long-term. These strategies are for illustrative and discussion purposes.

Ultimately, what strategy or mix of strategies will be most effective is dependent on numerous factors, many of which cannot be predicted with any certainty. Your nonprofit's specific Enterprise Strategy must be allowed to evolve and remain sensitive to those ever-changing external forces as the world and competition changes around you.

START-UP ENTERPRISE STRATEGIES

Every nonprofit begins somewhere. Typically, it starts in the mind of someone who identifies an unmet need and wants to be part of the solution. Maybe it's someone who has suffered a personal loss and doesn't want that to happen to others. Perhaps it's someone who has a mission, be it religious or ideological, who wants to give back to others. Start-ups are particularly vulnerable and either fail or go dormant at alarming rates, regardless of their goodness or purpose.

So, what specific strategies can be deployed to get newly formed startup nonprofits through their wobbly first years?

- Project a mission and purpose that is clear and compelling.

- Start local, then think global, by building a local base of committed advocates, volunteers, and small donors.

- Create awareness through local community media, clearly demonstrating they are here to stay by making the community a better, safer place to live and play.

- Actively participate in community events and establish a presence, not asking for donations, but seeking volunteers and building goodwill that will pay future dividends.

- Attend local government meetings and let them know the good things you are doing for your community.

- Keep expenses down and don't use credit cards to finance your good deeds.

- Demonstrate their commitment to the cause by putting their money where their mouth is.

- Keep volunteers close and treat them well.

- Work out mutually beneficial relationships with more experienced nonprofits.

- Connect with businesses and corporations with a history of supporting local nonprofits.

- Establish a presence in the community by utilizing the local news.

- Identify local philanthropists or community foundations. Don't start with a big ask; it's best to graciously accept a small donation that leaves the door open for more, rather than turn them off by being overly aggressive.

Now go do what you said you were going to do, do it well, and tell others about your good deeds.

Breakout Strategies

Breakout strategies are useful to organizations that have been around for a while but are either semi-comatose, in decline, or about to go completely dormant. Clearly, they need to re-energize their base (if any is left) and enhance their visibility. Now is the time for them to re-establish their mission, position, and purpose in their local operational areas.

- Run (don't walk) to the nearest business school or local nonprofit guru and request some free consulting, analysis, and advice. Business schools are particularly interested in providing student labor as a learning experience for both you and them.

- Focus on new opportunities and not on past missteps. At the same time, there needs to be a concerted review and effort to resolve both visible and "behind the curtain" people and structural and operational weaknesses that have been impacting performance. Leave no stone unturned at this stage. Identify your strong suit and lead with strength.

- Explore partnership opportunities with other more viable community nonprofits. Get back in the game.

- It's time to get your grant mojo going once again and seek funding opportunities from new sources or from those with whom you have had previous positive relationships.

Dust yourself off, pick yourself up, and start all over again. It might be time for new leadership at both the board and the operational levels and to reassess your outdated business model.

Stuck-in-a-Rut Strategies

Perhaps other life issues have intervened and you shifted your energy and assets to different causes, but now it's time to move forward.

- Don't take half measures by shifting resources away from what you do well to fix holes in what you do poorly. This is a recipe for chaos and ultimate collapse of the enterprise.

- Think, re-think, or reinvent who you are, what you do and how you do it. It's too late for half measures. Engage the entire organization in the analysis, identification, selection, and implementation of new strategies. There needs to be a buy-in for change if any change is to succeed.

- Mobilize the necessary resources and assets to sustain new enterprise directions and priorities. New strategies should be cycled in, fully integrated, and incrementally deployed.

- There will be resistance as you tinker and change your business model, such as replacing people with technology or cutting some programs and starting new ones. That gets employees, their unions, and their lawyers nervous, which can possibly derail all your efforts.

- Make sure you have an acceptable plan for redundant employees. For example, buyout packages, early retirement, retraining, and redeployment are some approaches to consider. If you don't have the appropriate mix of human or technological resources to achieve your new strategies, then make sure you factor those costs in; this is no time to back away from the "change is good" message.

- Remember, bureaucracies are notoriously inept change agents, so you must work extra hard to get everyone on board. Success with breakout strategies requires entrepreneurial thinking, enthusiasm for challenge, and a thick skin. While it won't be easy, if executed properly, it will be worthwhile.

Vacant or Specialized Niche Enterprise Strategies

Many larger, more established, and better funded nonprofits concentrate their development and marketing efforts on big funders with big money to fund big ticket programs. They do this because they can take advantage of economies of scale because they are competitive in this marketplace where entry costs are higher, proposal development is costlier, applications more complex, and the deliverables and time frames are more precise and unwavering. Then again, the payoffs and the awards can be in the mega-millions. Few can play in this marketplace except the major nonprofits with a national footprint, name recognition, and a track record of doing good with other people's money.

This creates vacant niche funding opportunities for other grant seeking nonprofits:

- If you can't run with the big dogs, then why not wait around to pick up the scraps? That's right, while the big guys are chowing down on the big dollars, there are literally tens of thousands of smaller grants, contracts, and awards out there that just might fit your business model.

- The Vacant Niche Enterprise Scenario is a marketplace ready for potential exploitation, in a positive way, by second- or third-tier nonprofits. Success probability is higher if the dominant players are off competing for the big stuff, allowing others to feed at the trough.

- Don't turn your nose up at the small grants—let's say from $10,000 to $25,000—because your first award is the most important one you will ever receive, regardless of the amount of funding, because it proves you can compete successfully. It allows you to build a track record and gets your foot in the door with donors.

Partnering-Up Enterprise Strategies

Community-based nonprofits tend to be small and focused around personal issues. Lacking resources, they have limited human and physical infrastructure—or public presence, for that matter. It's highly unlikely that nonprofits without a public presence or secure sources of funding can successfully elbow their way in and get a seat at the table.

Given this scenario, it makes intuitive sense to:

- Link or integrate capacities in some type of formal arrangement with larger, better-funded nonprofits, or form multi-unit collaborations with peer organizations.

- Be willing to consider a services contract, particularly if your organization has a unique capability and is in a yet-undeveloped market area.

- Merge the infrastructure and capabilities of several organizations, formally or informally creating economies of scale that would make these integrated enterprises more competitive. Not only are both risks and costs shared, merged organizations can execute multiple strategies.

- Limit financial exposure, expanding the reach, breadth, and capacities for considering merger and integration strategies.

Service Provider Strategies

When considering a Service Provider Strategy, keep these factors in mind:

- Contracts and fees for services are the primary funding mechanisms for service-type agreements.

- Local, state, and federal governments fund nonprofits to deliver a full range of services to eligible populations.

- Service Agreements are locally sourced and delivered by indigenous nonprofits, including faith-based organizations, schools, colleges, and universities.

- Examples of types of services provided include: health and wellness, day care centers, delinquency prevention, recreation, drug counseling, workforce training, and food distribution.

- The services can be as varied as the needs and requirements of the communities which are served.

- Service agreements are not "grants;" rather, they are "contractual obligations," typically requiring different operating models.

Competitive Advantage Strategies

It is difficult, at best, to be successful right out of the gate, no matter the field of endeavor. The competition has had the field of play to themselves for a while; they are a known entity and have successfully executed their mission. They have access to multiple funders who have been satisfied with their accomplishments. For the "new kids on the block," start-up and operational costs are just too high, so they often remain small or just fade away.

No one is immune to competition. How do you become that new presence on the grant-getting scene? Several competitive advantage strategies can be identified that can take you to that happy place where money flows and all is good with the world.

Below are several competitive advantage strategies:

- **Capacity Building**: While the competition is doing the "same old, same old," you're building capacity, slow but steady, step by step, adding new expertise, new technologies, improving facilities, and talking with donors about your new vision until you burst from the cocoon ready to compete and to win (to the surprise of your fellow nonprofits).

- **Modeling**: Some say imitation is the highest form of flattery, and maybe so, but this is another way to gain competitive advantage. That is, identify your competition, both those dominating the landscape and the ones left in their dust; perhaps your organization is one of them. Learn why some nonprofits are succeeding in the marketplace and others are not. Is it their relationship with the donors? Is it their expertise? Is it their constantly updated technologies? Their ever-expanding modern facilities? Their administrative and operational capacity? Now model what they have been doing, and yes, it might require changing things and investing money, but if you want to play you have to pay.

- **Pricing**: Cost and quality are the two most central factors in any award decision and critical to marketplace success. Some nonprofits have become overconfident by assuming the sponsor isn't price-sensitive and won't really care if they up the budget by 10%. Wrong. Very wrong, because you are in jeopardy of pricing yourselves out of the marketplace, believing your reputation and highly-placed advocates will carry the day. While the lowest price doesn't always win, the highest is always suspect and open to challenge. Sponsors, especially government sponsors, don't like to justify why they funded the higher-cost option when lower-cost options were proposed. Grant-getting is highly competitive, as you already know, and price can be one of those deal breakers.

- **Diversification and Innovation**: We have often heard the maxim "don't put all your eggs in one basket." A word to the wise: Don't become dependent on one (or even a few) source of funding and support. Keep investing in yourselves, growing your capacities, and refreshing your portfolio, always seeking new funding. By diversifying your portfolio, you are less likely to be discarded like yesterday's news when the sponsor announces a major change in priorities. Stay ahead of the funding curve. Likewise, it is never a good idea to be dependent on one sponsor for support, because as the world and politics change, the problems and the people change. Universities and nonprofits with a diversified base are better able to withstand marketplace swings and dislocations. Complacency and overconfidence can defeat you. The landscape is littered with the debris of once successful nonprofits who became overconfident and reliant on one or two donors.

- **Innovation:** All organizations must be prepared to intersect the future, and one sure way to do that is to make the future happen. It's called Research and Development (R&D). Nonprofits and universities can respond to alternate futures in two ways: lead the change and make it happen or be pulled along in its wake as an observer. Failure to allocate resources to future opportunities is not only shortsighted, but suicidal. Progress and change should not be left to luck or happenstance and our universities and nonprofits should not be satisfied with the way things are, but should strive to make them the way they ought to be. R&D is the vehicle for reaching a better future.

Dominance Strategies

You don't start out with a dominance strategy; you must first prove yourselves a worthy community partner to achieve a dominant position within your area of interest.

If properly executed, dominance strategies become almost self-per-petuating, but overconfidence can be a giant killer. You can neither sit on your hands nor expect your competitors to back off. It just doesn't work that way. How do I know? I have witnessed first-hand how one major university with a "national designation of excellence" let it slip away while competitors were developing new technologies and offering funders a more robust and advanced research capacity by creating a consortium of major players. The lone university could no longer successfully compete. Overconfidence was their undoing.

The Future Happens, Ready or Not

No matter how well you use these grant-getting strategies, both life and world events will have their way with you. We should never become complacent and start viewing life through the rear-view mirror. Grant- and contract-winning strategies that work today might not work tomorrow. Capacities, expertise, and technologies that are relevant today might become obsolete. Other nonprofits might choose to compete for the same funding opportunities. In other words, things change; the world changes, and if we don't remain agile, sensitive to the various environments in which we operate, and able to rapidly respond to shifting conditions, then we too can become irrelevant. Stay alert!

STRATEGIC DIRECTIONS QUESTIONNAIRE

Enterprise strategies are not conjured up, or picked from a hat; they are scrutinized, analyzed, tested, and twisted from every conceivable direction. Because if you think one of those huge cruise ships are difficult to turn, then just imagine what it takes to change the course of an organization. You must first understand where you are now and how you got yourselves there before deciding where it is you want to go and what enterprise strategies will get you there. Doing that requires insight, data, a plan, goals, and above all, honesty. Yes, honesty. If you shape the truth to protect your ego, you will end up at the same place: wondering why your organization is not successful while others thrive. That is why I have provided a Strategic Directions Questionnaire to guide you through the maze-like series of "what-if's" of organizational change. Don't focus on the past; rather, revisit your potentially new future. More importantly, get input from those closest to where the rubber meets the road; your staff, clients, and communities—those who have the most to gain or lose.

Please devote some quality time to this questionnaire because it will, if taken seriously, set you on a course that will yield positive results. It's a method for starting the discussion and for taking those incremental steps toward forging a new agenda and creating new organizational capabilities. Obviously, there are no right or wrong answers; only honest ones. Smaller nonprofits with singular or highly-focused initiatives should allow everyone to participate. Larger organizations with greater mission diversity and multiple departments, facilities, and initiatives, like colleges and universities, should have organizational sub-units reply independently and then re-aggregate those responses into a corporate-wide response.

Status

1. **Organizational Mission, Purpose, Goals, and Reason for Being:** Specify what you do (mission) who you do it for (clients), how you do it (process), and why you believe what you do is important to your clients. How does it contribute to the common good?

2. **Competitive Environment:** Identify competing organizations, locally or nationally, with similar footprints and missions that provide similar types of services to a similar client base. Be objective. Describe the competition and their facilities, expertise, funding sources, and approach to doing what they do by identifying what you are each better at doing and why.

3. **Financing:** What are your major sources of revenue? What percent of your total income comes from fees for service, contracts, grants, donations, and other sources? What is your "all-source" income? What do you do with it? If income is less than expenses, how do you bridge the difference? If you have multiple income streams, which ones have the most potential and why? How would your organization and its mission be impacted if income were reduced by 10%, 20%, or more? Do you have plans for such eventualities?

4. **Nonprofit Status:** Are you an independent 501(c)(3) or a sub-unit of a larger organization? If so, did the parent organization provide a cash subsidy or in-kind services?

5. **Grants/Contracts:** Where do you want to focus your energies? On grants, contracts, or fee for services? Did your organization ever apply for or receive a grant or contract? Do you view grants as an asset or more of a diversion while you'd rather focus on contracts? Are you planning on pursuing grant or contract opportunities in the near future?

Future

1. Do you have plans to expand your portfolio by diversifying your service mix, your client base, or by adding new locations? What are they?

2. If you have plans to diversify, would you consider merging with another nonprofit? Would you consider taking a secondary role, or would you insist on being the lead organization? Have you identified potential new funding opportunities? How do you intend on pursuing these? How do these new funding sources fit with your current or anticipated future capabilities, interests, and institutional mission? Identify each new potential funding source, why you believe the funder would be interested in supporting those new initiatives, and whether the organization is willing to invest its own resources to jump-start the process or to match funder dollars.

3. Do you have the necessary infrastructure, staff expertise, and in-place development capacity to successfully pursue new funding opportunities? Are you prepared to make those investments and strategic changes?

4. Are you willing to invest in new initiatives by redeploying existing resources or by hiring and upgrading facilities to operationalize those new initiatives? Do you have sufficient start-up funding to implement your new strategies?

5. Identify potential growth arenas. Do you have a plan for getting there? What is it? How much are you willing to invest? How would you characterize the major obstacles to entering this new marketplace? Would you rather collaborate or compete to gain access to the new operating arena?

STRATEGIC DIRECTIONS QUESTIONNAIRE

STRATEGIC DIRECTIONS QUESTIONNAIRE

Market Conditions and Opportunities

1. What is the market and sponsor environment for currently-funded projects or programs? Are they diminishing or expanding? If expanding, do you have plans to upsize or add new program components? If diminishing, how do you plan on maintaining your current market share and funding? Are you capable, with additional investment and effort, of taking a leadership position within this marketplace regionally or nationally?

2. How would you characterize the sponsor funding environment and their willingness and ability to fund new initiatives? Who are your target donors or funders for these new ventures?

3. Is there an existing or growing demand for your capabilities, expertise, services, or products? What is your funding conversion rate? Or, what percent of submitted proposals get funded? What immediate or long-term actions can you take to improve that ratio? Describe.

4. What "spin-off" programs, activities, and endeavors can be initiated to take advantage of your current competitive position, and what new marketplaces can be serviced?

5. How familiar are you (or your staff) with contract- and grant-supported programs in general and writing proposals specifically? What's your sponsor/donor development and grant-getting IQ? Do you need to recruit or hire-in new expertise? How do you reward successful grant getters within your organization? Are your project interests compatible with community perceptions, needs, wants, and expectations?

Organizational Competitive Readiness

1. Identify the type, quality, and quantity of competitors you must compete with in your area of endeavor and expertise for the same opportunities with the same donors. What organizations currently hold the dominant position locally, regionally, and/or nationally in those areas?

2. What are your organization's greatest strengths and advantages when compared to your competitors? Do you have the capability to leverage existing strengths into programs of local, regional, or national stature? Would it be more advantageous to turn competitors into collaborators by merging assets and resources? Are you willing to share intellectual property to create a regional, national, or international presence and footprint?

3. How do you perceive the future? Is it with confidence or trepidation? Why? What are the benchmarks of success? What programs and plans must be put into effect to achieve these future goals? Do you currently have the financial, technological, and human assets necessary to achieve these future goals?

STRATEGIC DIRECTIONS QUESTIONNAIRE

CHAPTER 9

Foundations: Who They Are, What They Fund

It's time to explore the wide world of foundations: who they are, what they do, how they do it, and the important role they play in the everyday life of nonprofits, faith-based organizations, schools, and colleges. Call them donors, call them funders, call them benefactors or good deed enablers; foundations are the ones that help make what nonprofits do possible.

WHAT IS A FOUNDATION?

A foundation is a nonprofit organization that supports charitable activities to serve the common good, as defined by them. Their funds come from endowments—money donated by individuals, families, or corporations. They rarely use principal to support their own ongoing activities, and make grants from the income earned by and from the investment of foundation assets. The IRS requires foundations to pay out at least 5% of the value of their investments every year, and if they don't, they are hit with an excise tax of 1-2% on earnings.

While most, if not all, federal donors follow the same rules, procedures, and guidelines regarding funding announcements, proposal formats and review and selection criteria, foundations have no compulsion to do the same. Thus, you should familiarize yourselves with each foundation's specific requirements.

Some foundations have more of a public presence than others, inviting general solicitations and making the public aware of their funding priorities. Others keep things close to their vests, notifying or inviting only selected organizations to submit proposals. Much like their federal counterparts, most foundations have pre-determined interests, policies, and funding priorities. They are, however, considerably far less complex in process and in practice, and generally have a more welcoming and accepting philosophy; this is now changing as larger foundations start following the federal model. It is the ease of submitting funding requests to foundations, and its openness to the community, that encourages the influx of proposals because, as many mistakenly believe, "if you ask for foundation money, it will come." In some circumstances, getting past foundation gatekeepers can be more difficult than obtaining federal dollars because they have far fewer dollars to award, are more difficult to locate, and can't levy taxes like their federal, state, and local counterparts to fund their good deeds.

TYPES OF FOUNDATIONS
Operating Foundations

As of this publication, there are approximately 4,574 operating foundations with some $42 billion in combined assets, giving or donating some $5.2 billion in an average year. These are the ones with name recognition, the type seekers read about and target because of their more robust giving portfolios. Many novice grant-getters think the more money a donor has, the more money they will give—well, that's not always the case. They behave, for the most part, very much like their public-sector counterparts, without the mind-numbing bureaucratic rules and regulations (with, of course, some exceptions).

Family and Independent Foundations

Most often referred to as independent foundations, they are the most common type of foundation, with some 73,764 registered independent foundations in the United States, with an estimated asset base of $540 billion. Many family foundations were created by successful family-owned and operated businesses. Sometimes these foundations were created for tax purposes, other times to support "family-centric" good works and favored charities, as well as to insulate themselves from unwelcomed attention. These foundations are closely tied to family fortunes and favor causes that are closely aligned with those family interests. Family foundations rarely have full-time staff, so intergenerational family members typically conduct the business of the foundation. The hard part is to locate them, establish contact, and then make your pitch. If given the opportunity to make a pitch, make sure it is consistent with family interests and priorities. There are sources of information available from the Foundation Center that can direct you to family foundations.

Community/Public Foundations

These types of foundations, more than 750 of them, have combined assets of $57.4 billion and award a combined $4.3 billion annually. They traditionally serve and/or operate for the benefit of a defined geographical area; they receive funds from a multiplicity of sources, both public and otherwise, and manage private endowments for donors who don't have the desire or the ability to start their own family foundations. Community/public foundations are administered by a governing body, or a "distribution committee," representative of community interests.

DISTRIBUTION OF FOUNDATION GRANTS BY SUBJECT CATEGORIES

Below is summary data from a national sample of 1,122 large foundations. While there are many more than this, here's an idea of what types of projects and activities foundations typically support and the levels of funding that comes along with those awards.[1]

- Arts and Culture: 19,882 grants averaging $177,947 per award, totaling $3.54B.

- Education: 28,439 awards averaging $176,418 per award, totaling $5.02B.

- Environment and Animals: 10,045 grants averaging $148,047 per award, for a total of $1.49B.

- Health: 20,176 grants averaging $338,421 per award, totaling $6.83B

- Human Services: 40,286 grants averaging $86,433 per award, totaling $3.48B.

- International Affairs: 3,534 grants averaging $196,138 per award, totaling $693M.

- Social Benefit: 16,980 grants averaging $132,520 per award, totaling $2.25B.

- Science and Technology: 2,775 grants averaging $192,894 per award, totaling $535.28M

- Social Science and Economics: 1,164 grants averaging $200,667 per award, totaling $233.59M

- Religion: 4,526 grants averaging $104,136 per award, totaling $471,32M

- Other: 65 grants averaging $106,149 per award, totaling $6.9M.

Grand Totals: 147,872 grants, totaling $24.54B

---

1   www.foundationcenter.org/findfunders/statistics/pdf04_fund_sub/2011/10-11pdf

IMPRESSIVE NUMBERS

The numbers are quite impressive; lots of awards and lots of money. *It should be a no-brainer to get my nonprofit funded,* you think. Well, let me give you a reality check. The Ford Foundation receives 40,000 proposals every year. That's right, 40,000. They give about 1,400 awards, for a conversion rate of 3.5%. Not very good odds, indeed. You would be better off buying a lottery ticket. This is the reality you will be facing when seeking foundation funding. It's hard, but not impossible, to obtain foundation funding. It takes acumen, persistence, and effort, as well as compatible interests, proof of concept, and recognition as a "premier" nonprofit in your area of endeavor, and connections wouldn't hurt, either. But play on, because you represent a worthy cause and there is foundation money out there waiting.

GETTING IN THE DOOR

While it is sometimes difficult to arrange personal meetings with foundation officials, for much the same reasons as federal agencies, there are other ways to get information. The Foundation Center conducts workshops and conferences for organizations and individuals interested in seeking and obtaining foundation funding. Many foundations, particularly the smaller ones, don't regularly publish or distribute materials describing their priorities and the areas they are interested in funding or generally reach out to nonprofit organizations. On the other hand, most of the larger and more publicly-known foundations have robust websites that are fully descriptive as to the form and process of applying for a grant in their selected areas of funding interest.

CORPORATE FOUNDATIONS

Giving away money is not the prime mission of corporations, large or small—making money is. Businesses and corporations must first create profits before they can give them away. Most corporations fully recognize their role and place in the community, and that "good deed doing" is an adjunct to building customer and brand loyalty, especially for local businesses. If the corporation prospers, then the corporate foundation prospers, as well. Corporate giving is typically delegated to their surrogate, corporate foundations. Some corporations, however, support direct giving programs in locations where stores or production facilities are located. Walmart is the ultimate example for doing good with other people's money, maintaining active direct giving programs in some 5,229 localities where Walmart stores and distribution centers are located, forming a *bond* in the communities where they operate.

The beneficiaries of local corporate and business largess tend to be local nonprofits such as the United Way and Red Cross, or the cultural community as represented by local theatres, the fine arts, and historic preservation. They try to stay as neutral as possible. Some corporations will match employee contributions to selected causes and organizations and encourage community volunteerism by giving employees paid leave. Companies with a national giving footprint often restrict their giving to organizations and causes in areas where stores, factories, warehouses, or regional headquarters are located. Communities with a surplus of successful corporations and businesses are truly fortunate, and this is one of those circumstances where geographical proximity works in their favor.[2]

RECRUITING INFLUENTIAL BOARD MEMBERS

Gaining access to senior corporate staff can prove difficult. Such forays are usually handled by public relations staff. Requests for support are responded to politely, but are deftly turned away or referred to their Foundations, which were established to both formalize the giving process and to distance themselves from giving decisions. If local businesses or corporations do financially support local events, organizations, and charities, the next step for grant-seekers is figuring out how to "press the

---

2   www.mcf.org/nonprofits/what-is-a-foundation

flesh" or get a personal meeting with the decision makers controlling the flow of money to worthy causes.

There are two primary approaches to gaining access. First, try to identify what individuals, politicians, community groups, friends, and relatives are connected to the business you want to approach. You know, the ones who "know people." Do this without calling in too many chips, because the next time the welcome mat might not be out; and you now owe them one. When asking for support for any good cause, be sensitive to the politics of the request; that is, can this cause be linked to positive outcomes such as good press and new customers or business opportunities? Giving is a two-way street. Be sensitive to the competing demands and the surrounding business environment. Clearly demonstrate, in as precise a way as possible, not only the importance of the gift and the cause, but the potential benefits the business or corporation can realize from its support, particularly in terms of public image.

Second, bring the corporate, business, and political worlds into your fold. Seed your board with representatives of the corporate and political worlds. Prospective board members are asked to serve for many reasons, but high on the list is personal donations or access to the movers and shakers (and their money). This is easier said than done, because many board prospects are up to their ears in offers to join boards, because they know the game, too. They can be quite guarded about what community and organizational boards they will serve on and lend their good names to. The nonprofit must have real relevance to the potential board member; or, at least, the mission shouldn't cause them embarrassment. Another approach is to drop down to other significant people. If you can't land the CEO, ask him to nominate someone else in the organization—someone who can't refuse the invitation. And don't forget elected government officials or non-elected bureaucrats who control the public's purse strings. Be aware, however, there are conflict of interest laws which might preclude some from supporting funding; that is, if they have direct ties to the dollars. Be creative in composing boards, because they are critical to every development effort. Also, be aware of the interlocked nature of many community boards and be prepared for those "pulls and tugs."

BUSINESSES AND CORPORATIONS CAN DONATE MORE THAN MONEY

There is yet another side to the business of giving. More than money can be donated; there are many valuable assets that corporations can and are often willing to share. Human assets, for example, such as experts in finance, technology, and marketing, can provide wise counsel. You might also ask for and receive deep discounts for supplies, products, or access to facilities that have lain dormant. The extent of what a local business or corporation can give (and you can utilize) is only limited by your needs and the creativity of your requests. Please keep in mind that they do not like to court controversy. They want to invest in programs or charitable activities that have broad public support—ones that will not reflect poorly on the donor organization.

WHAT CORPORATE FOUNDATIONS FUND

Foundations typically make these types of awards to selected nonprofits, faith-based organizations and schools: (a) capital grants which support the purchase of property, the construction of new facilities, or the rehabilitation, remodeling, or expansion of existing facilities; (b) endowments which are a permanent annual source of income; (c) unrestricted grants that allow nonprofits to direct funds wherever it is most needed; (d) project grants financially support specifically identified initiatives and activities that advance the foundation's interests; and (e) challenge or matching grants which encourage the nonprofit to leverage additional funds and not solely rely on the donor for all its needs.

A HORSE OF A DIFFERENT COLOR

Foundations are typically as guarded as federal donors in allowing access to funding decision makers, for the right reasons. They do not want to treat potential applicants differentially in the name of objectivity, although we all know that can sometimes be an elusive goal. Unlike federal funding, there are fewer hoops to jump through. Foundation submission requirements, along with their complexities, are often scaled down compared to the time-consuming and almost indecipherable rules, regulations, documentation, and certifications government submissions require. Foundations don't see value in requiring submitters to devote substantial time and resources to writing overly complex proposals packed with all sorts of conditions and certifications, as do federal agencies; especially in a relatively low probability acceptance environment.

Many foundations prefer short form proposals, or what I call "screening proposals," to determine if it fits the donor's funding profile. The submitter does not have to devote countless hours to researching and writing proposals, and the foundation does not have to devote too many human assets to reviewing them. Based on screening reviews, the foundation invites selected nonprofits to submit a full proposal. Both doer and donor save money and angst. It's a much more efficient sifting process because the funder does not have to slog through potentially hundreds of lengthy and off-the-mark proposals to find those diamonds in the rough. And seekers don't have to devote substantial time, effort, and expense in writing proposals with little probability of success. Everybody wins; figuratively, that is.

Some foundations conduct community workshops open to "all comers," and I would advise that, when offered, you attend as many of those as possible. That is where you can ask questions and gain insights to what the foundation sees as their funding priorities. Once funded, the relationships change; that is, you will typically be assigned to a program or project manager that will stay with you through the duration of the funding cycle.

PROFILE: THE WALMART FOUNDATION

Let's look a bit deeper into the giving priorities and behaviors of the mega-retailer, Wal-Mart, and their donor policies and strategies. The Wal-Mart Foundation funds only nonprofits and subdivides its giving categories into four segments: national giving, state giving, local giving, and international giving, funding only nonprofits in each of these four sectors. However, Wal-Mart only accepts "invited" international giving proposals.

The National Program

This program awards national grants starting at $250,000 to nonprofits with a national footprint, focusing its interest on social issues across the United States, primarily in these areas: hunger relief and healthy eating, sustainability, women's economic empowerment, and career opportunities. The initial application for funding is made through a Letter of Inquiry (LOI) rather than a full proposal. LOIs are screening mechanisms that ultimately benefit both submitters and funders.

State Giving Programs

Grants in this category typically range from $25,000 to $250,000 and have their focus on underserved populations, however they define it. Wal-Mart has empowered State Level Advisory Councils, consisting of Wal-Mart employees and associates, to review funding requests and to make funding recommendations. There are two annual funding cycles, applicants must be nonprofits and either be state affiliates of national organizations or have a statewide presence. Applications are submitted online.

Local Giving Programs

Wal-Mart, according to their literature, believes in operating globally but giving back locally and having a positive impact in the neighborhoods where employees live and work. Through the local giving program,

Wal-Mart and its affiliated organizations award grants of between $250 to $2,500 through each of their local stores and operating entities. The local stores have the authority to make those grants, so this might be a good way to literally get your foot in the door. Donations can also include food or other products. Applicants, once again, must either be nonprofits, government entities, educational institutions, or faith-based organizations. Applications must be submitted online.

CORPORATE GIVING'S TOP TEN

- Wells Fargo: The nation's largest mortgage lender donated some $315,845,766 in cash with a focus on housing. The largest grant was $77 million to a nonprofit called NeighborWorks America as part of the bank's NeighborhoodLift initiative, which provides down payment assistance to low income residents and funding to stabilize cities and neighborhoods most affected by the housing crisis and foreclosures.

- Wal-Mart Stores: Donated almost $316 million in canned foods and $756 million in products, including 421 million pounds of food, and provided support to 50,000 charities primarily through grants made by local stores.

- Chevron Corporation: Donated some $262.5 million in cash, with the largest grant of $11 million going to the Niger Delta Partnership as part of a four-year, $25 million commitment to promote economic development and fight poverty in Nigeria.

- Goldman Sachs Group: Donated some $241.2 million and funded a $100 million five-year company initiative to help women start businesses in the developing world.

- Exxon Mobile Corporation: Donated $256 million in 2012, with the largest grant of $22 million going to support their National Math and Science Initiative and $3 million to Vital Voices Global Partnership supporting the Business Woman's Network in Africa.

- Bank of America Charitable Foundation: Donated $186.8 million in cash and $36 million in products to support critical initiatives facing neighborhoods and communities, awarding over $22 million to more than 650 nonprofits addressing housing needs.

- The JP Morgan Chase Foundation: Donated $183.5 million in support of improving the lives of the under-served global community, particularly in cities and communities throughout the world in which they have clients or an operational presence.

- The GE Foundation: Donated $161.5 million to find solutions to some of the world's most difficult problems, with a focus on health, education, environment, and disaster relief.

- Target Foundation: Donated $147 million with an emphasis on bringing cultural opportunities into schools, supporting nonprofit organizations that encourage kids to read, and the arts and social services in communities where Target has a presence, particularly the Minneapolis-St. Paul area.

- Citi Foundation: Donated $137 million in support of community enterprise development and microfinance, youth education and employment, and neighborhood revitalization.

There's probably something of interest here for every nonprofit; the question then becomes, is it worth the time, effort and money to go after those high-profile opportunities, or are there "easier pickings?"[3]

FOUNDATION OPPORTUNITY SEARCH ENGINES
Foundation Directory Online

The Foundation Center developed and supports a foundation-specific search engine called Foundation Directory Online. This is a proprietary product of the Foundation Center and is the premier database for any nonprofit, public charity, school, or organization interested in seeking

3   www.philanthropy.com/article/10-Companies-That-Gave-the/140261

foundation and corporate foundation funding opportunities. This subscription database is updated weekly, providing, according to the Foundation Center, the most comprehensive and accurate information on U.S. foundation grant makers and their funding activities. Searches can be conducted by county, metropolitan area, and zip code, as well as by city and state, with many options for saving and sorting opportunities. There are different levels of subscription, from Basic to Professional. The Basic Level offers key facts on America's 10,000 largest foundations by total giving, as well as identifying 73,000 foundation trustees, officers, and donor names. The Foundation Center maintains nine comprehensive databases reflecting all grants made by listed foundations and 990's, which are IRS-required foundation filings from which the Grant Center culls much of their contents for the databases. The search engine also includes RFP's (Requests for Proposals), over 108,000 listed foundations, corporate donors, and grant-making charities, over 3 million recent grants, more than 500,000 trustee, officer, and donor names. If you can't afford a private subscription, many local libraries subscribe to the Foundation Directory Online, which patrons can access without cost.

The Grantsmanship Center

The Center offers members access to Funding State-by-State, a database identifying grant-makers, including foundations, community foundations, and corporate giving programs in the areas where nonprofits operate. They also maintain *GrantDomain,* a database of foundation, corporate, and government grant makers using key words and phrases. For more information, go to www.tgci.com. This is a paid or a subscription service.

SAMPLE FOUNDATION PROPOSAL TEMPLATE

- **Executive Summary**: The summary should be laser-focused on the proposal's key points, including problem, proposed solution, funding requirements, and organizational capability and experience.

- **Statement of Need:** Three paragraphs informing the reader about the issues; facts and data demonstrate the criticality of the need and how it impacts real people

- **Project Description:** A compelling statement describing what you are going to do, why you have chosen this approach or strategy, and how you are going to do it.

- **Objectives:** Identify anticipated outcomes, deliverables, and real measurable improvements you expect to accomplish by the conclusion of the program cycle.

- **Methods:** What strategies, tactics, methods, and processes will you deploy to achieve identified outcomes and deliverables, and in what time frame? Also, include why your approach will work when others have failed.

- **Staffing/Administration:** The types and numbers of required staff, including their skills, work experience, educational achievements, specific duties and functions, and how they will be integrated into your organization.

- **Evaluation:** How you will measure project progress and success, including what metrics you will use and who will make those assessments—a staff member or an independent third party?

- **Sustainability:** How you will maintain project activities after the funding cycle has ended. Does your organization have a history of successfully attracting external funding for similar types of activities and projects?

- **Budget:** Identification of the proposed project's financial requirements and costs, the "reasonableness" of those costs and whether the requesting organization will provide either cost share, or contributed time and effort to support the project. Will there be any anticipated revenues?

- **Organizational Information**: History, mission, structure, focus, current programs and activities, board composition, and populations targeted.

- **Conclusion**: Bringing it all together in your final pitch—why should they fund your organization and project when there are so many other needs?

- **Transmittal/Cover Letter**: Every submitted proposal should be accompanied by a Transmittal or Cover Letter. It must be signed by an authorized official, such as the Chief Executive Officer and perhaps the Board President, indicating that this is an official submission of the XYZ nonprofit and follows funder (name of the organization) requirements. Identify the funding opportunity applied for and a short, not overly hyperbolic, statement as to why your organization should be considered for funding. Congratulations, your submission is now complete!

As you can see, the Foundation and Government proposal templates are similar in format, with the primary difference being the depth and complexity of the required responses. As previously indicated, foundations much prefer a screening approach, allowing them to reduce the time and effort of all involved. Based on screening proposal reviews, the foundation staff or donor will invite selected nonprofits to submit a full proposal containing much of the same detail as what a government sponsor would typically require. So please familiarize yourself with Chapter XX: Why Some Succeed When Others Fail. And good luck!

CHAPTER 10

Idea First, Money Next

FINDING THE MONEY IS EASY– GETTING THE MONEY ISN'T

I t all begins with "the better idea." There is nothing more annoying and off-putting to a sponsor than a seeker shrieking, "Where's the money, where's the money?" Donors are not in the business of randomly giving out money or responding to perceived past transgressions. Rather, they are in the business of supporting worthwhile efforts of every type and variety consistent with their interests and priorities, while the seeker must prove, one way or another, that their idea will add to the sum and substance of making the world better.

The first thing you need to have is the better idea; how to mediate or resolve a recognized but unresolved need or problem. Provide a critical but missing service, like housing the homeless. Above all, keep this reality constantly in mind. Donors don't give funds because you are needy; they give funds because you want to help the needy and make this world a better place one family, one block, one community, one state, and one nation at a time.

Finding the money, winning those awards, getting those donations is the challenge that confronts every nonprofit, big, small, or in-between. Like everything else in life, it's a process; a very complex one.

While it is always preferable to meet with donors face-to-face, it is particularly difficult to arrange, especially with federal donors, because they have very strict protocols about with whom they can meet, particularly when there is an active Request for Proposal on the street. Oftentimes, they will have "open meetings," where anyone interested in submitting for an opportunity can meet with a government official. Bottom line, a contract or grant officer cannot give information to one applicant without providing the same information to all potential applicants. It's a pain, but if strictly followed, it creates a level playing field for all. While most donors, for public purposes, encourage openness and contact, they typically only provide access through some type of written document and refer inquiries to their websites (which identify their areas of funding interest, as well as the processes and requirements for accessing and entering their world). Sounds easy, doesn't it? Regardless of your good intentions, getting other people's money is one of the most stressful, competitive, high-stakes activities outside of professional football. I know, because I have the scars to prove it.

ONLINE SEARCHABLE DATABASES: APPROACH WITH CAUTION

A brief note and disclaimer: I am providing detailed information on specific databases, primarily those with broadest applicability. The government-sponsored databases identified here offer free access, but you must register. There are privately-sponsored search engines offering additional features (at a cost), and you might want to explore them, as well.

Avoid, at all costs, "the sponsor trap." Much like a beautifully designed spider's web, it lures the unsuspecting into a sticky tangle of threads from which few will emerge. Just as in the animal kingdom, it is the uninitiated that end up as a protein snack. The sponsor trap is easily sprung on the starry-eyed novice grant- or contract-seeker. The bait, in this instance, is the plethora of online sites and books (yes, this is a book) that promise to show you where the money is buried and how you will unlock the funding treasure chest. "It's easy," the charlatans scream at you from infomercials; all you need do is send off a letter requesting money for some worthy cause and patiently wait and wait and wait, and then wait some more. Of course, in your heart of hearts, you know the old saying, "if something sounds too good to be true, it probably is," but, I guess hope springs eternal, and the hopeful often get fleeced.

Information and sources of funding are ubiquitous if not always accurate or current. If these online sources are available to you, they are also readily available to the tens of thousands of other money-seekers out there. There is no competitive edge here whatsoever, and it is, after all, the competitive edge that makes you a winner.

HAVE A PRE-PLANNED SEARCH PROTOCOL

The explosion of technology has made it easier than ever to hone in on all the numerous databases out there; some you must pay for and others are free, but all have their strengths and weaknesses. I am also from the "leave no stone unturned" tribe, so I suggest cross-referencing among these various databases. It is a good idea to have a pre-planned search protocol with types of funding opportunities and key search words already in hand. I am also from the school that it is better to consider all close-fit opportunities the first time through and then sift them through a finer filter to narrow the search to the most probable. In other words, be more inclusive rather than exclusive, because opportunity identification and selection is a critically important first step in getting other people's money.

BE BOTH PATIENT AND THOROUGH

A word of caution: while some of these opportunity databases are easily traveled, others require a bit more thought, particularly those developed, maintained, and hosted by our friendly federal government. Be prepared to be confused, because many of these searchable databases are wrapped in "government speak," including the indecipherable enabling legislation creating these opportunities. Be patient. You will find yourself, at first, questioning your competence and perhaps your sanity. Eventually, you will learn this new language. I guess that's the price of entry into the federal treasury.

When reviewing funding opportunities, carefully note each sponsor's contact information, the available funding opportunities, and the dates when RFP's will be officially released, as well as the dates that proposals must be submitted with all those pesky representations and certifications completed and certified. The submission requirements alone are enough to send you packing, but persevere. Carefully, very carefully, read, review, interpret, and interpolate all that "donor speak" to come up with a short-list of opportunities that square, not only with the nonprofit's need for funding, but with your expertise, experience, interests, and capabilities.

Make specific note of the funding authorizations for each of these opportunities (which could be in the millions or hundreds of millions), the average or maximum amount of funding, how many awards will be made, in what geographical locations, and award duration. If the submission dates don't allow you enough time to research, write, prepare, package, and fully review a truly compliant and competitive proposal, then move on to something else, one offering sufficient preparation time. The last thing you want to do is submit a less than fully-vetted and compliant proposal to a sponsor you want to do business with in the future.

GRANTS.GOV: LET THE GRANT SEARCHING BEGIN

Anyone interested in searching thousands of opportunities can go directly to www.grants.gov. This is the "Thousand Pound Gorilla" of grant websites, consolidating grant opportunities from almost every federal agency into one accessible site. It also offers user guides and checklists, training videos on how to use the site, how to register, how to find and search efficiently for grant opportunities, and how to obtain your required DUNS number, provided free by Dun and Bradstreet. Registration is required if you plan on submitting your grant application directly through grants.gov.

I call it the "Federal Goody Book." This is your portal into the world of federal funding. Grants.gov was created to provide a website to find and apply for federal funding opportunities. It houses information on more than 1,000 grant programs for 26 federal grant-making agencies and awards more than $500 billion annually. While you do not have to register with grants.gov to search for grant opportunities, you do have to register if you intend on applying. The process takes between 3-5 days.

According to the grants.gov website, the benefits to using them are: (1) they centralize more than 1,000 grant opportunities for 26 federal grant making agencies; (2) they facilitate interaction with the federal government by streamlining the grant process and by allowing you to register only once to apply to any of the 26 listed federal agencies; (3) they simplify the application and submission processes by using a single electronic portal; (4) they allow for simple keyword searches for grant opportunities from all 26 agencies; (5) they make electronic grant application processing easier and more intuitive; and (6) they provide a secure and reliable source to apply for federal grants. Sounds good, but let me tell you, it isn't as simple and easy as they want you to believe; remember, we are talking about the U.S. government.

Stay Focused

It is important to remain focused on opportunities that are consistent with your organization's interests, capabilities, and experience and not be diverted. As you cycle through the website, you will perhaps be entertained, and at times confused. And, don't forget to go to agency-specific websites to make sure you have gathered every important bit of information. Individuals are not eligible to apply unless they represent an "eligible organization" as described below.

Organizations Eligible to Apply for Grants Through Grants.gov

- Government organizations, including local, state, city, or townships, special districts, governments, and Native American tribal governments.

- Educational organizations, including independent school districts, public- and state-controlled institutions of higher education, and private institutions of higher education.

- Public Housing Organizations, including Public Housing Authorities and Indian Housing Authorities.

- Non-Profit organizations having 501(c)(3) status with the IRS.

- For-profit organizations and small businesses fitting Small Business Administration definitions and standards.

- Individuals can submit for opportunities but are only eligible to submit for opportunities open to individuals and cannot submit on behalf of a company, organization, institution, or unit of government.

Grants.gov also makes a very interesting disclaimer; we have all seen them: late night infomercials, websites and reference guides, and advertising millions in free money. Don't believe the hype! Although there are many funding opportunities on grants.gov, few of them are available to individuals and none of them are available for personal financial assistance. It clearly demonstrates how far unethical people will go to steal from those in financial distress.

Federal Agencies Offering Grant Opportunities Through Grants.gov

- Agency for International Development
- Department of Agriculture
- Department of Commerce
- Department of Defense
- Department of Education
- Department of Energy
- Department of Health and Human Services
- Department of Homeland Security

- Department of Housing and Urban Development
- Department of Interior
- Department of Justice
- Department of Labor
- Department of State
- Department of Transportation
- Department of Treasury
- Department of Veterans Affairs
- Environmental Protection Agency
- Institute of Museum and Library Sciences
- National Aeronautics and Space Administration
- National Archives and Records Administration
- National Endowment for the Arts
- National Endowment for the Humanities
- National Science Foundation
- Small Business Administration
- Social Security Administration

All Federal grants must be officially announced to the public. It will not show up in your morning newspaper or on television and radio. You should be proactive and continually search the website, since opportunities are continually being rotated. Each grant announcement contains instructions on how to apply, including where to get an application packet, the types of information the application must contain, the date the application is due, and agency contact information. There is no single document that contains every federal grant announcement and no uniform format for these announcements. In addition to grants.gov, most grant announcements are listed in the Federal Register, a daily publication that is available on the internet and at most public libraries.

If more assistance is required, most federal agencies have grant specialists available to help organizations apply for and manage their grants. Applicants are urged to call the contact identified in the grant announcement or contact the regional office. Agency staff are available to answer questions over the phone—and good luck to you. Remember the saying, "I'm from the government and I'm here to help you."

Almost every type of organization can apply for opportunities through grants.gov but a note of caution, especially to the uninitiated: be prepared, as I have previously stated, for a mind-bending experience.

CATALOG OF FEDERAL DOMESTIC ASSISTANCE (HTTP://WWW.CFDA.COM)

Catalog of Federal Domestic Assistance (CFDA) is another federal database that you should become very familiar with. It was the grant-seeker's Holy Grail until the release of grants.gov in 2002. It provides additional information and agency insights not included in grants.gov, including background documents such as legislative authorizations, fiscal details, accomplishments, regulations, guidelines, eligibility requirements, information contacts, and application and award processes. It is repetitive in some ways with grant.gov, but you get a bigger picture and more detail, which might give you a greater understanding of the agency's mission and, more importantly, a competitive edge. The CFDA contains descriptions for some 2,300 assistance programs and a full listing of all federal programs available to state and local governments, federally recognized Indian tribal governments, territories and possessions of the United States, domestic public, quasi-public, and private profit and nonprofit organizations and institutions. Its primary purpose is to assist users in identifying programs that meet specific needs and objectives of potential applicants. It contains financial and nonfinancial assistance programs administered by the various departments and agencies of the federal government. The CFDA is managed and maintained by the General Services Administration in coordination with the reporting agencies. Opportunities can be searched by agency or category. Use this to cross-check the information from grants.gov; it might just provide insights that may save you a lot of time (or it could reinforce your decision to move ahead with a grant application).

AGENCY-SPECIFIC FEDERAL GRANT WEBSITES

I suggest you use grant.gov as your primary opportunity source locator and note the agency and opportunities you are interested in. Then go to the agency-specific websites to determine if there is additional information and insights that could help you make a decision.

Some agency specific addresses are provided:

- www.hhs.gov/grants/US: Department of Health and Human Services grant and contract funding opportunities

- www2.ed.gov/fund/grant/find/edpicks.jhtml?src=Ln: US Department of Education (USDOE) grant funding opportunities website

- www.neh.gov/grants/index/html: National Endowment for Humanities (NEH) grant funding opportunities website

- www.USAID.gov/partnership-opportunuities/respond-solicitation

CHAPTER 11

Money! Money! Who's Got the Money?

FINDING THE OPPORTUNITY THAT'S RIGHT FOR YOU

Donors hold your future in their hands, because Doers are dependent on their money and their willingness to share those monies. They, in turn, depend upon the nonprofit to use those funds for their intended purposes and to accomplish the mutually agreed-to goals and outcomes. Is this a balanced relationship? Probably. There are certainly mutual interests and shared concerns patched together with a degree of reciprocity and mutual admiration. That is, when everything works out according to plan. What really makes it work is the clearly demarked division of responsibility. Donors have the means and a vision of what this "better world" should be like, and nonprofits have the infrastructure, the knowledge, ideas, and capability to turn that vision into reality (at least, that's the way it's supposed to work). Sounds like a fair trade. While there are no guarantees in life, there are protocols to be followed, suggestions to be considered, and best practices to be tried. All these taken together provide a roadmap to the place you've so longed to reach—that is, doing good with other people's money.

IT'S TIME TO STOP DREAMING AND START DOING

Today, identifying potential donors is relatively easy; all you need is a rudimentary knowledge of computers, easy access to the internet, a keen eye (to separate the real from the fraudsters), and patience, lots of patience. Seeking funding for your good cause is more involved than just looking for dollar signs along with the names and addresses of funding organizations ready to entertain a proposal. The outcome we all hope for is that the donor will be so blown away by what they read that a check is already in the mail. Unfortunately, that's not the way it works. So stop dreaming and start making good things happen.

IT'S ABOUT WHO YOU ARE AND WHAT YOUR ORGANIZATION CAN DO

I will say this now and I will say it repeatedly: Winning grants or contracts is not about search engines or about the stacks of sponsor web pages on our desk all promising instant millions. It's about who we are, what we do, how well we do it, and who benefits. It's about our accomplishments and contributions to society writ large. Ultimately, it's about the donor and whether they value our vision for making our nation and world a better place. The plan is then packaged into a proposal and submitted to a potential sponsor for their review and assessment of worth. If the sponsor sees the world through the submitter's eyes, the proposal will most likely be funded. Once final details and understandings are worked out, agreements or contracts are executed, then high-fives are the order of the day. Now, the awardee must shift from proposal mode to operational mode and focus on outcomes and deliverables, because the ball is in their court. No excuses, no blame game, because it's delivery time. Words must now be translated to actions, and those actions must advance the outcomes that you promised to deliver. Congratulations! And that, in a nutshell, is how it all goes down.

TEN ATTRIBUTES OF HIGHLY SUCCESSFUL GRANT-GETTING NONPROFITS

So, let's go back to the original premise: how do you become a "lean, green grant-getting machine?" There are ten essential attributes grant-centric nonprofits must possess if they are to succeed in the highly competitive world of doing good with other people's money.

Successful grant- and contract-winning organizations exhibit the following common qualities and characteristics with varying intensities of emphasis and strength:

- **Professional and Committed Workforce and Leadership:** Fully engaged and committed to the organizational mission and purpose, highly trained, collaborative, knowledgeable, client-centered, and grant-savvy.

- **Clarity of Mission and Purpose:** Ambiguity is not part of their vocabulary—they know what their strong suit is, what they do best, where they are headed, and what they're going to do when they arrive.

- **Multi-Functional Capabilities:** Agility, diversification and adaptability are all part of their organizational DNA. Their multi-faceted skill sets allow for quick pivots when necessary.

- **Reputation for Excellence:** Clients seek them out, peers model them, funders bring opportunities to them, the competition avoids competing against them, and they've become the go-to nonprofit for advice and counsel.

- **Resilience:** They exhibit the unique ability to quickly deal with or recover from unanticipated disruptions and events, marketplace shifts, or funding dislocations—they "take a licking and keep on ticking."

- **Proximity:** Always wanting to be part of the solution, not the problem, they are intimately familiar with impacted communities and their hopes, needs, and wants.

- **Innovativeness:** Willing to leave their comfort zones and always ready to explore new approaches and solutions to recurring and broad-reaching problems, wherever they occur and whomever they impact.

- **Relationship Building:** Never underestimating the value of relationships, especially with those controlling the money. They prefer to build connectivity one person at a time and weave them into mutually supportive networks.

- **Treat Failure as a Learning Experience:** Success is neither guaranteed nor inevitable. If they fail, they pick themselves up, dust themselves off, and start all over again. They know something many don't know—that failure is ultimately the mother of success, and we don't want to disappoint our mothers, now, do we?

- **Execute:** Possess the strategic and tactical capacity to quickly move from theory to practice and adroitly execute any planned project, mediation, or intervention within cost and without drama or disruption to the organization.

How many of these essential attributes does your organization currently possess? Be honest, because you can fool yourself into believing you are ready to compete for other people's money, but you won't be able to fool the donor. Donors are not only reviewing and assessing proposals; they are putting your organization under a microscope, as well. You must prove your worth before getting their money. Donors are especially cautious when considering whether to fund untested nonprofits. They want to understand who you are, what you do, and how you do it to determine if your organization is grant-ready. You'll get there, but do it the right way and don't apply for funding before you are fully competitive and confident that you can *say what you will do, and then do what you say*—I told you I would repeat those lines.

THE FUNDING ANNOUNCEMENT: YOUR INVITATION TO THE PARTY

It's time to do some "opportunity mining," this time at a desk. Think of the program announcement or Request for Proposal, as the starting point. It's your invitation to the party; the beginning of a possible relationship.

There are two critically important distinctions that MUST always remain firmly planted in the back of your minds every time you even consider applying for grant or contract funding:

- First, it's easy to identify deep-pocket donors, but it's extremely difficult to separate them from their money, unless, of course, you know the "secret handshake."

- Second, inexperienced grant- or contract-seekers chase dollars, but successful grant and contract getters build relationships and reputation then let the dollars find them.

Before getting stuck in a web of donor confusion take these somewhat offhand pronouncements seriously. It will save you time, cost, and flailing about (and most of all, turn funding "no's" into funding "yes's").

A NECESSARY, BUT NOT SUFFICIENT CONDITION

Identifying funding opportunities is a necessary, but not sufficient condition for winning awards. It is, however, a task that must be done and be done well. Novice grant- and contract-seekers must learn how to separate what is a real funding opportunity from what I call a Trojan Horse Opportunity, which is an announcement that appears to be a real opportunity but is crafted in such a way that only one organization, or just a very few, qualify to compete. In other words, to distinguish between openly-competed funding opportunities and funding opportunities that have a history of being awarded to specific types of nationally-recognized or politically-savvy nonprofits.

Don't be shocked, but donors have ways of directing funding opportunities to specific organizations. Experienced grant-getting organizations are aware of these types of tactics and have probably benefited from them themselves. So, before any effort is expended on a potentially lost cause, the first thing you need to do is determine if this is a real funding opportunity or not. I started my grant-getting career in the poverty program where I had no previous experience in these matters. This form of government legerdemain was really driven home when I had a meeting with the nation's longest-serving mayor, who said to me, "Son, people like to do business with their friends." The message was received and understood.

MANY PATHWAYS LEAD TO THE SAME DESTINATION

There is not only one, but rather many pathways to becoming successful grant- and contract-getters and creating financially sustainable grant- and award-driven organizations. The focus should be on outcomes, not procedures; on substance, not flash. Grant- and contract-seekers are always being observed and evaluated because this is one of the few activities where the bottom line is readily observable. Either you win the award that you spent so much time and energy on, or you don't. Learn from every failure.

Stay the course, whether you are an individual, a small nonprofit, or a major university, because as grant and-contract seekers you have the power and the knowledge to solve problems, turning ideas into actions. Most of all, you are on the front lines of making the world better, one proposal at a time. As with all things, it takes money (lots of it) to accomplish even the most valued of society's tasks, and you are the bridge between those dollars and the people they will help.

TO SUBMIT OR NOT TO SUBMIT— THAT REALLY IS THE QUESTION

Writing winning proposals is the name of the game because no one sets out to write losing ones. But it happens more likely than not. Many so-called funding experts typically using templates and encourage nonprofits to write numerous proposals, assuming one just might sneak through. The even more unscrupulous among the tribe charge often-desperate organizations (some on the brink of failing) large fees for pre-written or "boiler-plate" proposals that never won anyone anything. Such approaches don't work and these "experts" are only expert in their ability to separate you from your money. Their real purpose is to make money from you, not for you. YOU need to write the proposal, because who knows more about your organization and what it can do than those dedicating their lives to helping others?

So how do you decide what opportunities are worth pursuing and what opportunities are not? And even more importantly, if you are competitive for a specific funding opportunity? Not having this information would just be a waste of time.

IT'S ABOUT FIT, COMPATIBILITY AND COMMON INTERESTS

Don't just wander through funding opportunity search engines; that is both a waste of time and a clear indication you are new to the game and haven't read this book. Yes, you will find hundreds of interesting funding opportunities, and some might even match your interests. They will take you on a merry chase unless you have a search plan and a funding focus. From a strategic perspective, I recommend that your search focus concentrate on identifying donors who financially support organizations that resemble yours in terms of size, types of activities, and issue orientation. That is, they have a history of funding the types of initiatives your organization is known for and has competently delivered year after year. Below is a list of essential information and criteria you should be focusing on to assist you in determining if you are "competitive" for a specific donor opportunity:

ARE YOU COMPETITIVE?

If you can answer "yes" to questions 1-7, add that donor to the "follow-up list." Repeat the process for every donor you believe to be a good fit. Once you have compiled a funders list, move on to questions 8-12. As indicated, you might have to go to specific donor websites to obtain the requested information.

1. First, is your organization eligible to submit for funding opportunities from this specific donor?

2. Second, what are the donor's primary funding interests? Do these areas of primary interest match up with your interests, capabilities, and previous experiences? Do you believe you would be competitive for these opportunities?

3. Third, can you achieve required outcomes and deliverables within the financial envelope proposed by the donor?

4. Fourth, do you possess the requisite experience, facilities, staff, program, and delivery capabilities the donor expects you to have in place?

5. Fifth, do you have donor-required financial, administrative, and reporting infrastructure, including a recent financial audit (please note a recent "clean financial audit" is often a requirement particularly for federal funding)?

6. Sixth, consider the types of organizations this donor tends to fund: Large well-funded nonprofits with name recognition? Medium to small organizations? Local/state government entities? Professional organizations? Nonprofits such as grass-roots neighborhood and community groups? Child-focused organizations such as schools?

Faith-based organizations? Colleges and universities? Does your organization fit with any of these descriptions?

7. Seventh, what are the application protocols? Consider the date by which proposals must be submitted. Are proposals restricted to specific issues and concerns? Are there specific submission formats that must be followed? Can your organization prepare a well-vetted, professionally written and content-rich proposal within the submission deadline?

DONOR SPECIFIC INFORMATION

If the information for any of these questions is not readily available in the funding opportunity search engine, go directly to the donor's website. Cross-reference the website with what you found on the funding opportunity search engine. Do this for each viable funding opportunity. In other words, become intimate with their websites.

Now, with the additional information in hand, respond to questions 8-10:

8. Eighth, how are proposals reviewed and selected for funding? What are the criteria used? How many grant requests and proposals are submitted in an average year, and what is the aggregated funding percentage? What are typical funding ranges, from low to high?

9. Ninth, if possible, calculate the organizations's award rate percentage. (Many provide that information.) It would typically be expressed as a percentage of the number of proposals submitted. Based on the probability assessments associated with each funding opportunity, identify those that have the highest funding percentages. Now prioritize the ones you believe are "most probable" from a fit and funding perspective for your organization. Is a 20% funding rate worth the effort? How about 5%? Or 30%? What about a 3.5%

success rate? Where do you draw the line? Or do you believe you can defy the odds because you are better at the grant-getting game than "those others"?

10. Tenth, perform an "environmental scan" and prepare a list of possible competitors for each potential funding opportunity within your geographical area who are also potentially eligible to apply. Compare strengths and weaknesses, along with track records, and ask yourself, *who would the sponsor select, if given a choice?*

11. Eleventh, if all the input and data, funding success probabilities, and unbiased analysis indicate that you are competitive, get that proposal writing group cranked up and ready to go.

12. Twelfth, given current staffing and expertise and available funding opportunities, how many competitive proposals can you submit in a year? Do you have the capacity and infrastructure to apply for and manage two, three, or even four separate grant awards from potentially different donors? Because that is what it will take to create a financially self-sustaining grant-funded enterprise.

CAN WE TALK?

When you factor in all the variables, including the competition, the real costs (in time, dollars, and effort in writing a competitive proposal), and funder probabilities, you now have objective data to assist you in making a "go or no-go" decision. I know, *I'll be one of the winners,* you think and want to believe. You are correct, but neither is it a wise decision to ignore the laws of probability. It's your time, effort, and money, so *you* make the decision. Oh, and buy that lottery ticket.

Four Grant- and Contract-Getting Takeaways

1. First, above all, understand that grant- and contract-getting is part art, part protocol, part bravado, part salesmanship, and all intellect—in equal portions!

2. Second, grant and contract getting has become ritualized and formalized, allowing for limited flexibility and interpersonal contact between submitter and funder. The proposal is the most important commodity and the primary vehicle for conducting business.

3. Third, flexibility and agility are essential attributes of successful grant- and contract-getters. You need to understand the funding environment in which you are working, the strengths and weaknesses of the competition, and your probabilities of success before you even consider whether to devote money, time, and effort to a specific opportunity.

4. Fourth, your ultimate success as a grant- or contract-getter is as dependent on creativity, intuition, style, personality, capability, determination, and the exercise of good judgment as it is on following every rule, procedure, protocol, and bureaucratic mandate. While a high value is placed on consistency, it is often battered by contradictions, and ultimately, it is the insightful understanding of these antagonistic dynamics that leads to funding success.

CHAPTER 12

Getting Your Organization Grant- and Contract-Ready

ORDINARY JUST DOESN'T MAKE IT

Ordinary doesn't make it in this highly competitive and complex world of grant and contract giving and getting. Organizations must present themselves as problem solvers who deliver and as the go-to place for solutions to what ails their communities. The proposal needs to represent both your unique capacities and how you will resolve identified problems or felt needs.

IT ALL STARTS WITH THE FUNDING ANNOUNCEMENT

Is This an Opportunity Your Nonprofit Should Pursue?

Before diving in to the grant pool, determine if this is the right opportunity at the right time. If not the "right one," then let it go! There will be many more to follow. You can make a "go or no go" determination by simply answering these questions: First, is this funding opportunity within your wheelhouse and does it fit your organizational experience profile? Second, do you have a competitive advantage, and what is it? Third, is this a high-need community concern?

The drill remains the same, regardless of funding source. That is, before making any decision or jumping to conclusions, a thorough review of the announcement is required. The general rule of thumb is to not even consider applying for an opportunity until you have the most current funding announcement and have confirmed it is, indeed, an "active opportunity." For example, if you see a foundation opportunity in a search engine that looks interesting, then you should go to the foundation's site to see if it is posted there. If it is, dig deeper into the priorities of the foundation and familiarize yourself with their program interests and funding protocols. Analyze the types of projects previously funded and what types of organizations typically won those grants. You can never have too much information, because moving forward without due diligence can lead you down a blind alley with the simultaneous loss of time and money. Once determining the announcement is the most current and hasn't been withdrawn (or the deadline passed), read it, read it again, and perhaps again.

Funding announcements go by many different naming conventions. Call them RFP's (Request for Proposals), RFQ's (Request for Quote), CFP's (Call for Proposals), Program Announcements, Grant Announcements, Grant Notices, Funding Opportunities, Notice of Grant Opportunities—they are all vehicles for letting interested parties know what types of funding opportunities are out there. The technology for searching and locating potential funding opportunities has gotten easier in some ways and more difficult in others. More difficult, because you are inundated with funding opportunities; each one bigger than the next, or more interesting than the last. Novices can easily get overwhelmed by the plethora of opportunities and blinded by the huge sums of money donors have available.

WHAT FUNDING ANNOUNCEMENTS TYPICALLY INCLUDE

Funding announcements typically include all the necessary forms, such as what organizations are eligible to apply and budget templates, as well as certifications and representations that must be agreed to and executed by submitting organizations. The announcement may also include any combination of the following: the nature and purpose of the award, what the funding can be used for, identification of key proposal components (or a model proposal outline); funding authorizations and specific guidelines, including the number of maximum pages, font size, what is to be contained on the cover, and even how budgets are to be prepared and displayed; when the proposal must be submitted; and to whom it must be submitted. It is within the announcement that you may also discover how proposals will be reviewed and selected for funding. The announcement may state what types of activities can or cannot be undertaken.

Mine the announcement for every nugget of information you can. Read between the lines, because oftentimes there are key words which should give you a heads-up; sometimes it's what is *not* said that is more important than what *is*. Be fully aware of the announcement's implied or inferred meanings before you input word one. The announcement might also provide some insights into who your competition might be. Take the announcement quite literally; don't put your own spin on it, or you just might find yourselves doing a heck of a lot of work for nothing. Pay close attention to the funding organization's goals and priorities, the self-identified needs or problems this sponsor wants addressed, the types of awards to be made, what geographical areas they cover, their general terms, conditions, and requirements for applying, and the average award size.

CAN YOU SUBMIT A CREDIBLE PROPOSAL WITHIN THE IDENTIFIED TIME FRAME?

Is your staff capable of doing two jobs? That is, their "day" job and the new job of writing a responsive grant proposal without either suffering? The proposal is the common denominator—it's your admission ticket to the world of "Doing Good with Other People's Money." It's how we compete against other nonprofits and how we inform the donors about our capabilities, our good ideas, better ways of doing things, and how we can make our communities a better place. The proposal must focus on what advantages, capacities, and assets you can offer the funder, not what you need from them. It's not about you; it's about what you can do for others. It's been a long run up to this the final stage of the grant-getting process, so it's now time to focus on writing a winning proposal. Since nothing is simple in the world of doing good with other people's money, why should the proposals be any different?

WHAT DONORS EXPECT FROM DOERS
Coordination and Collaboration

Donors are particularly interested in funding collaborations and partnerships. Some donors have shifted their funding priorities and approaches gravitating from their "old" funding model (that is, funding major community institutions such as schools and museums) to spreading a little money around to the more numerous local nonprofits and faith-based organizations for both political and logistical reasons. This shift had unintended consequences, creating in-fighting, separate fiefdoms and competition among the smaller nonprofits, rather than coordination. The focus has now shifted to funding nonprofit networks reducing overhead, complexity, infighting, and donor costs. At the same time, services get expanded. Donors, indeed, like to save money, but they also like to reduce their administrative burdens as well.

New Ways of Solving Old Problems

Don't follow the herd with the same old, same old. Find new solutions to intransigent problems that work. Donors don't fund innovation for innovation's sake; they, like the rest of us, are seeking answers to deeply-rooted problems. Whether social, environmental, economic, or technological —you put a name to it and some organization, somewhere in the world, is pursuing it (some more aggressively than others).

Always Ready to Rock n' Roll

Another way of winning the hearts and minds of donors is to be ready to go at a moment's notice without having to purchase new equipment or hire additional resources; this is counterproductive from a funder's perspective. They don't want to pay for new equipment and purchase new technology for every grantee unless it is essential to conduct the project. Donors are aware of that game, and some require nonprofits to turn over any equipment purchased with sponsor funding upon project completion, which they can then redistribute to other nonprofits. It's best, from a competitive position, that nonprofits remain agile and always ready to pursue the next funding opportunity.

Location, Location, Location

Most donors and funders like to do business with people and organizations they are familiar with; the ones who have delivered consistently on time and within budget. While many "Requests for Proposals" are national, they typically reference local capabilities. Funders often prefer to fund local nonprofits with deep knowledge of the people living in impacted areas. Communities, and the people within them, are often resistant to working with new and unfamiliar organizations that come into their neighborhoods and say, "We're here to help you!" They have heard those words many times before. Local organizations that have, perhaps for decades, been "plowing the same fields" are more trusted. Local nonprofits have a built-in advantage when competing for funding because of that local bias. That is why location can be a big advantage when competing for donor funding.

Make an Offer They Can't Refuse

Having the right answers, the right capabilities, the right connections, and the right pricing strategies are powerful grant and contract winning strategies. Don't stray too far from your funders and keep reminding them you are out there, ready for their call. Your friends will still be your friends and funders who have had positive experiences with your nonprofit will likewise be predisposed to providing new funding opportunities. This is your opportunity to make new friends or attract new funders—particularly those who have yet to recognize your strengths or those who have yet to fund you. If they are not fully aware of who you are and what you do, then make them aware of your capacities and good deeds. Make them a deal no one else is prepared to match. Yes, you can use pricing as a lever. Sometimes establishing new sources of funding requires you to suck it up and bid at the low end or simply underbid the competition—this is particularly effective when competing for contracts. By demonstrating what you can do and proving it in real time, you will be at the head of the line when new awards are made.

Telling a Compelling Story

A proposal, in its purest form, should tell a story. It should tell a story of hope, of people, of ideas, of discovery, and of new ways of doing things; about what the future would look like if your nonprofit were funded and allowed to deploy its solutions. It's at the writing stage when all those concepts you want to test must now be integrated into a coherent story containing three critical themes. First, a need must be identified and its significance demonstrated. Second, the proposer (that's you) must clearly articulate and demonstrate that they have a plausible idea to resolve a longstanding problem and their approach is innovative and unique, yet practical. Third, the nonprofit must clearly demonstrate it has the experience, competence, capacity, and capability to make it happen. All these components must be woven into a well-written, professionally presented, clear and concise proposal fully responsive to sponsor requirements and priorities.

WHAT DONORS DON'T WANT: OVERPROMISING AND UNDER-DELIVERING

The proposal should describe, in varying amounts of detail, what is supposed to happen, over what time frame, what the outcome(s) will be, how much it will cost, and, how the nonprofit expects to accomplish all this. The proposal is a representation of what the submitter expects to accomplish. It is a self-defeating strategy to knowingly make unrealistic claims or promise outcomes you know cannot be achieved just to make you appear more competitive. Always respect the intelligence of the sponsor; they've seen it all and heard all that "pie-in-the-sky" stuff. Puffery, especially in a proposal, will come back to bite you. It is always in your best interest to realistically represent your capabilities, what you intend to achieve, and how you will implement your unique approach.

That is why much thought, time, and effort must be focused on writing the proposal and why so much importance is placed on reviewing proposals. There are so many filters, reviews, and submission requirements; that is why so many proposals are rejected and so few funded. The kiss of death, to which many nonprofits fall prey, is what I call the "overpromising and under-delivering syndrome"—so prevalent, yet so easily spotted. Whether done naively, out of inexperience, or purposefully, to outshine the competition, it is a losing strategy for your organization and for the community you are committed to serving. So, don't do it!

KNOW WHAT YOU ARE APPLYING FOR

I previously provided the U.S. Government's legal definitions of grants, contracts, and cooperative agreements. Now let me use some more user-friendly explanations. Many mistakenly use the terms "grant" and "contract" interchangeably or the term "grant" as a generic term for all types of awards made by a sponsor (whether government, corporations, or foundations). "Award" is a commonly used term for a grant, contract, or cooperative agreement. So, without muddying the water too much, if I said, "We won a federal award," it would have little meaning if I didn't specify whether we were awarded a grant, contract, or cooperative agreement.

Grants have grown more rule-laden over time; originally the money was provided and the awardee went off and did their thing with little fear of consequence. Today, grants require the execution of grant agreements, and if you understand even 50% of the terms and conditions, you are ahead of the game. In other words, they are becoming more like contracts. Contracts are the preferred vehicle when government needs to either acquire services or products to keep the U.S. Government and all its facilities and personnel operational. It does bind both government and nonprofit to the accomplishment of specific deliverables, whether services or products. Failure to provide agreed-to deliverables can be harmful to the pocketbook if a nonprofit or for-profit fails to achieve mutually agreed outcomes. Cooperative agreements, another type of contractual instrument, is part grant and part contract, giving local or federal officials a seat at the table. In other words, they are directly involved in how the awardee carries out the activities of the cooperative agreement.

GRANT READINESS QUESTIONNAIRE

It's now time for another questionnaire. The answers to these questions might just help you win that first award or stop you from wasting valuable time and energy chasing your tail.

How do you know when your nonprofit is ready to apply for grants or contracts?

- Have you applied for and/or received IRS 501(c)(3) status?

- What awareness does your community have about your organization and its mission, purpose, and contribution to the community? Who would miss your services or suffer most if you closed shop tomorrow? What would they miss most? What would they miss least? How would local government react to your shutdown? Would they provide emergency funding?

- Narratively and demographically describe your catchment area. How would you categorize and describe the most pressing problems facing your community and its residents?

- Are you fully operational and capable of managing all aspects of donor funding? Do you have the necessary administrative, financial, technological, human, and delivery infrastructures in place?

- Do you have sufficient income to maintain organizational operations and pre-fund a project start-up? Do you have sufficient financial reserves to weather either loss of an existing grant or a reduction in funding? How long can you maintain operations if funding were to be reduced or withdrawn?

- Have you identified your organization's sweet spot within your community of focus? Are you currently being donor funded? Do you have a better idea for how to solve some of your community's most pressing challenges and intractable problems?

- Do you have a business plan? Are you following it? Are you where you want to be—why or why not?

- Do other nonprofits in your catchment area have similar capabilities and capacity? How would you rank them as a competitive threat—high, medium, or low?

- Are leadership and board members recognized community members? Do they have access to the other power brokers within the community, including government, business, nonprofit, and educational sectors?

- Can you document the impact of current and former programs? How have they measurably improved the lives of community residents? Be specific.

- Do you have or seek collaborative arrangements with other community nonprofits? Who are they? Be specific.

- Do you have a future vision for where you want the organization to be within the next three years? Are you sufficiently diversified to survive changes in donor funding priorities?

- Are your facilities adequate for the programs and projects currently operational? Can current facilities accommodate potential growth? Are they close to your primary clients and customers? Are they accessible by public transportation?

- Can your organization quickly ramp-up if new funding opportunities present themselves?

- What stage organization are you? Start-up (0-1 year), newly established (1-3 years), or mature organization (3+ years)? How many years have you been operating under your current corporate charter?

- How many different funding sources do you have? Specify if you receive funding from different income streams, identifying the sponsor or the source of income. What is the average annual income received from each?

- Do you have a mission that allows for growth and expansion, or is it narrowly defined?

- Do you have recognized and strong leadership? Qualified and respected staff and an effective board? How would you characterize the community's willingness to support your organization?

If you could answer "yes" to fourteen of the eighteen indicators, you are ready to go for your first grant, contract or award. Good luck to you!

GRANT READINESS QUESTIONNAIRE

CHAPTER 13

Writing Winning Proposals

TURNING WORDS INTO ACTIONS

Moving an idea from concept to implementation is the ultimate test for any organization wanting to do good with other people's money. It's easy to write a proposal and describe a "new world order" where everyone is equal, well fed, educated, nonviolent, and law abiding, almost like Minnesota's mythical Lake Woebegone. But it's extremely difficult to turn concepts into funded realities and then actually accomplish what you proposed to do.

There are many forces at play in the world of doing good with other people's money. Those responding to a funding opportunity without fully understanding how the grant and contract game is played will more than likely fail. Success requires you to both understand and meticulously follow the sponsor's rules of the road.

ARE YOU COMPETITIVE?

Realistically speaking, reviewing and deciding what grant or contract opportunities you will respond to requires an honest assessment of your organization's competence and capabilities. Whether funders agree with that assessment determines if you will be funded or not. Donors learn from good deed doers, and good deed doers learn from donors and what they value. New ideas, approaches, and tactics to resolving solution-resistant problems are always welcomed, but not always funded, regardless of how hard you worked developing and researching your new idea. Funders, particularly federal ones, give more weight and credence to prior experience than to yet-untested organizations proposing unconventional solutions. I know, sad but true.

DO YOU HAVE A SEARCH PLAN?

Create a search plan, otherwise you will be overwhelmed with information not knowing what opportunities are real and what opportunities are not worth pursuing. Those just getting into the sponsor funding arena should realize that entering this club is neither easy nor obvious. Don't just focus on the big names. Rather, look for the smaller, more locally focused donors, those the experienced players have already graduated from. Carefully review each announcement and website and look for the nuggets of information that might just give your unique idea an advantage. Read the website and then read it again, because it is your key to eventually unlocking their doors and overcoming the barriers that are sometimes purposely erected to keep the uninitiated out, at least by some funders. You still have much work to do, but be assured the result will be worth the effort for you and those you want to benefit.

DOING GOOD IS THE EASY PART

"Doing good with other people's money" probably didn't even make our Top 10 when we had that "what are we going to do with the rest of our lives" moment. Many of us who experienced the tumultuous 1960's heeded President Kennedy's call to the youth of our nation, "Ask not what your country can do for you, ask what you can do for your country." That world view has shifted, dramatically so, but many still seek to help others and be part of the solution, not the problem, gravitating to those professions allowing us to follow such a path. Now, fast forward to today and here we all are, about 13.7 million of us, working in the nonprofit sector; some 10% of the American workforce, supported by almost 63 million dedicated volunteers who do their good deeds without compensation.

WHAT'S YOUR VALUE PROPOSITION?

You see, "doing good" is the easy half; it's the "with other people's money" part of the equation where we all struggle. In the private sector economy, we exchange money for something of value around which a need or want has been created, whether it's a car, a refrigerator, the vacation of a lifetime, or that shiny new bicycle.

In the nonprofit sector, what exactly are we exchanging our hard-earned dollars for? Let's get back to the original proposition—what are we exchanging? What's our "value proposition" when asking for other people's money? Typically, we are appealing to or attempting to energize the innate desire within most of us to help others, or what is called altruism. We sometimes overplay our hand using emotionally provocative messages to trigger the altruistic tendencies of potential donors, which ideally causes them to open their wallets. We have all witnessed those horrific scenes of starving children in Africa because not enough of us out there care enough to save those precious little lives. Sound familiar? There are better, more authentic ways to activate our giving instincts.

SHOW ME THE MONEY

The Federal Government funds some $500 billion in grants and contracts annually. These funds are typically awarded to 501(c)(3) organizations, governmental sub-units, colleges and universities, public charities, nonprofits, and faith-based organizations. And what about the approximately $600 billion in block or categorical grants? They make up 17% of all federal expenditures made to the states or other publicly eligible sub-units and entities. Some of these block-granted funds find their way into the coffers of nonprofits.[1]

---

1   www.grants.gov

SOME GIVE, MANY RECEIVE

So, let's add all this up: individuals, corporations, and foundations donated $358.38 billion to various good causes.[2] The federal government annually awards some $500 billion in grants and contracts to eligible nonprofits, charities, colleges and universities, public and private schools, and school districts and $607 billion is block or categorically granted to states and local governments. My best guess total is that some one trillion dollars in funding is potentially available to nonprofits, faith-based organizations, local and state governments, and other sub-units of government to improve the lives of its citizens. Even if my addition is somewhat off base, this is not a trivial amount, I assure you, and is well worth your time and effort to pursue. This is your opportunity to help others realize their dreams with a lot of help from individual contributors, government, foundations, and corporations. But first, you must get very good at playing the grant-getting-game.

STATE GOVERNMENT FUNDING OPPORTUNITIES

Don't think for a minute that state governments aren't big players in the grant-giving and -getting game. They are the recipients of block grants and revenue sharing courtesy of the Federal Treasury. States then move this funding down the chain to counties and cities, but hold on to a big chunk for their own use. In addition, they put their tax dollars to good use by contracting with nonprofits and faith-based organizations, as well as private sector businesses and corporations. I am most knowledgeable about New York State and its approaches to funding schools, nonprofits, and faith-based organizations. I am sure every state in the union has similar interests and funding opportunities. What I found interesting was New York State openly admitted that nonprofits were being buried under a mountain of paperwork, with 75% of the contracts executed late, burdensome requests for documentation, and late reimbursement

---

2   http://www.givinginstitute.org

payments. New York State committed to simplifying their management protocols, streamlining contract processing for nonprofits, committing to timely payments, and in general transforming their business practices. In response, New York State created a Grants Gateway, created a Master Contract, went to multi-year financing, and allowed organizations to prequalify. They identified the nonprofit/state government friction points and created solutions. Kudos to them! Oh, and if you think this is small stuff, think again, because New York State and its 33 agencies awarded over $1.2 billion via their new system and the Grant/Contract Gateway.[3]

MAKING OPTIMISM YOUR CO-PILOT

Our actions and decisions have consequences, and in the world of grant-giving and –getting, some will succeed and others will not, but optimism is always your ally. Perhaps you won't win that grant or contract the first time out, nor perhaps the second, but if you are prepared to learn and persist, you will ultimately prevail. So, don't be put off by the competition, because your cause is as worthy as theirs. Remain energized and challenged by them and then try and try again because that is what it will take. Be The Little Engine That Could, not the one that wouldn't.

SAMPLE GOVERNMENT PROPOSAL OUTLINE

Proposal formats used by government organizations, particularly at the federal level, typically contain these primary component parts in this order.

Proposal Abstract or Summary

This are the first words reviewers will see and read. These words can, and most likely will, shape the reviewer's opinion for the rest of the document. So, make sure the summary establishes a positive and realistic

---

3   www.grantsreform.ny.gov/

tone. If the summary is unable to fully convey the strengths of the ideas and the merit of the execution plan, the proposal review process might just end there. The summary is your first and best opportunity to establish your place in the funding universe; to create your voice, tell your story, and manage expectations. It is an overview identifying the overarching purpose of the project and its anticipated goals and outcomes or what will be improved after the project has completed. It also indicates how the efforts can be sustained once funding ends. The summary is the last thing you write and let me reiterate that—after the proposal has been fully vetted and internally reviewed. I recommend the summary be written by someone with limited or no involvement with preparing the proposal, allowing fresh eyes to view the document. After all, it is the reviewer's fresh eyes that will be reading and ranking the proposal and determining whether it is fund worthy or not. If the abstract does not align with the rest of the proposal or fairly represent what the reviewer will encounter reading the rest of the proposal, this can quickly become a problem. Don't oversell or hype; if there are issues that must be addressed or data that must be collected, make sure those issues are represented in the abstract. If the perceptions of how the author of the abstract views the proposal is wildly or even moderately different from what the writing team intended, there is a discontinuity that must be reconciled before, not after, the review.

Organizational Background and Experience

This component is your opportunity to formally present your organization to the donor. Think of it as a coming out party. Some nonprofits have instant name recognition, many do not. Sometimes name recognition can be a positive, particularly if the nonprofit has a national profile, is known in the community as a reliable friend, or is a major employer, such as a college or university, that brings prestige and national recognition to a community. Reputation can be a double-edged sword, especially for those nonprofits that have failed to build positive relationships within their communities or have run afoul of the media.

Describing your organization's *background and experience* is an excellent platform for creating synergy between the Donor and Doer. It's your opportunity to demonstrate common cause and concerns and to establish credibility, or why you believe your approaches are best positioned to implement the specific donor-funded program. You might go on to say that it's about structural change, not temporal solutions. Likewise, it should describe the organization's goals, philosophy, strengths, and track record in the community and with other donors. It's a good place to recognize community collaborators and demonstrate your community's overwhelming support for this project. It's vital to create a common vision for this "better place" and that you see the world through the same eyes as the donor. You need to gain complete buy-in by outlining how, through collaboration with others, assets can be combined and leveraged. Don't use this section to trash your competition, particularly with unsubstantiated or otherwise false comparisons. That typically doesn't go over well with donors.

Problem Statement

The problem statement is the most critical proposal component. It is from the problem statement that all else derives: objectives, technical approach, personnel, budgets, and so on. Above all, do not even attempt to sway the Donor by parroting back your potentially mistaken impressions of what a donor wants to hear. If the donor had the answers, why would they be expending large sums of money and valuable time to find alternative solutions to unresolved challenges?

A sound, fundable proposal starts with a sound, fundable problem. The problem statement must be clear, concise and compelling. It *must* be supported by data and seconded by others in the community. It should clearly identify what the problem is and who is impacted. It needs to include your initiative's relative importance when compared with other extant problems and what you plan on doing about it. It is the foundation of the "ask" (or why you are seeking grant funds) and why you believe this problem is worthy of donor funding. Avoid trivializing the problem, thinking you could lure the donor in to believing you had the answer in your back pocket. Nor should you sensationalize the problem as if the world would end tomorrow if it were not immediately resolved. Don't rehash the same old dog-eared approaches that have been tried multiple times with little success. It is a sure bet that if a problem has been around for a long time, most conventionally held ideas have already been tried. When this type of stalemate persists, donors are more willing to both consider and fund out-of-the box solutions.

Project Goals, Objectives and Deliverables

After a fundable, coherent and attainable problem statement has been identified, attention should turn to project goals, objectives, and deliverables. Clear, meaningful, measurable and intuitively logical objectives are important, not only to the sponsor, but to project staff as well. It not only provides a measurable framework, but also is a way of tracking progress and where the project is in time and place. Now is a good time to clear up some confusion, especially as it relates to the difference between an objective, a goal, and an outcome. Goals refer to anticipated long-term results. An objective, on the other hand, is the delivery of a specific result, product, or service within a specified timeframe. A goal might be to enhance the quality of life for the elderly living in public housing within a specified community, and a collateral objective would be providing two healthful meals for the elderly seven days a week. An outcome would be to reduce the incidence of diabetes in the identified elderly population by 50% within 12 months. Surrounding the proposed goals, objectives, deliverables, and outcomes should be a timeline detailing when specific actions and activities will be achieved, including the all-important objectives, goals, deliverables, and outcomes.

Work Plan

The work plan, sometimes referred to as the *technical work plan*, describes how your organization will go about achieving those objectives, goals, outcomes, and deliverables. You are strongly urged to include and discuss alternative approaches and why you chose the one you selected. You need to clearly demonstrate to the sponsor that you know what has been tried, what has succeeded, and what has not, and why your approach will succeed where others have failed. Demonstrate how this approach can be scaled-up to larger communities and populations.

The work plan should (a) specify how all those objectives, goals, outcomes, and deliverables will be accomplished; (b) detail timeline(s) for achieving deliverables and outcomes; (c) identify target populations and how they will benefit; (d) identify what the social and economic impacts of the project will have on the community; (d) provide alternative approaches that have been considered and state why you selected the proposed alternative; (f) what additional resources (human, technological, and financial) will be required to successfully engage this problem; (g) name collaborating partners and experts you have enlisted in this effort and how they will contribute to a positive outcome; (h) provide an organization chart identifying current, and proposed new project positions, including reporting relationships and which individuals will be charged directly to the grant; and (i) outline what assets and other "in-kind" services you can get from the broader community to augment your activities such as free consulting services, volunteers, and free or low-cost goods and services to demonstrate buy-in.

Project Organization and Management

After project objectives have been identified, alternative approaches reviewed and selected, activities listed, deliverables and outcomes fully characterized, and timelines firmed up, it's time to integrate all these varied processes into a coherent management plan. Donors don't like paying for overhead; they typically want all their funding to go to operational project funding. Most of all, they want their money to go to those in need of services. Here are some more caveats:

- Keep project management and organizational structure clean and simple. Complex doesn't work. Neither does spending money on expensive technologies, particularly if you cannot prove their value to the project. This might be a way of gaining vendor support, but you will first amuse, and then lose, donor support.

- Clearly demonstrate the purpose of each new position requested. Explain why the position is needed and what it will do. Outline how it will contribute to project outcomes. If additional personnel are deemed critical, then you also must demonstrate how these new employees will be absorbed into the organization once funding ends.

- Funds are rarely awarded to either rent or purchase new facilities and equipment, particularly new office furniture, unless it is critical to project outcomes. It smacks of a personal enrichment; a way of using other people's money to feather your own nest, not helping others.

Project Assessment and Evaluation

Donors not only expect the proposal to include clearly stated and achievable goals, objectives, and deliverables, but also require recipients to file periodic reports detailing program progress. The donor wants to know what metrics you intend on using to measure program outcomes and progress and why those metrics were chosen. They want to know how they will contribute to the effectiveness of project performance, what worked, and most importantly, why. If there is project drift, what midcourse corrections are required to get the project back up to speed? How do you intend on avoiding those mistakes as you go forward? The evaluation plan should not be an afterthought or something you ignore or don't take seriously. Donors must go back to their boards or bosses and prove the funding was well spent and deliverables were achieved and identify who did a good job with their money.

Good intentions are not enough to attract follow-up funding, but successful outcomes and provable results are. A definite willingness to prove your worth and to provide progress data sends a message to the donor—one that says *we know what we are doing and we are willing to prove our approach works*. Donors will sometimes reserve the right to conduct independent program and/or financial audits to ensure that sponsor funds were expended for appropriate purposes. Keep in mind they also reserve the right to conduct program audits if they find your efforts lacking. So, take the program audit and reporting requirements seriously; your future funding may depend on it.

Donors also want to know what project goals and benchmarks were achieved and which ones came up short and why. They want to know why you succeeded in some areas and not in others. Was it because you did not have an effective marketing program, or was it because it was a very cold and snowy winter? They may ask what factors helped you and what factors hurt you and what new approaches you will deploy to do better in the next quarter. The sponsor will compare your project results with those you so confidently placed in the proposal and so strongly defended in the personal presentation. The sponsor will compare actual outcomes against anticipated outcomes identified in the proposal and calculate the delta between what was proposed and what was accomplished. They'll think about whether you closely monitored project progress or not, and if not, why. Just because you are a nonprofit doesn't mean you are not responsible for the outcomes; quite the contrary. You now have a public obligation, particularly if you were funded from public sources.

Budget and Cost Sharing

The size, purpose, and scope of the budget must be consistent with what you have agreed to accomplish. It's very easy to pad budgets and even easier for reviewers to find that padding. While awards are somewhat cost sensitive, it does not always follow that the lowest cost offer will carry the day. Rather, it is the organization presenting the most compelling proposal to resolve that unresolved problem that are the most competitive. There are two reviews—one review focuses on the project plan and approach and the other examines cost factors and whether they are reasonable or necessary. Even if you under-budget on the hope you will be the low bidder, you will still be held accountable to those agreed-to objectives and outcomes. Even more importantly, past performance is a predictor of future success.

Be realistic in your financial expectations and needs. I suggest a top-down budget approach. This method requires that both programmatic and budgetary decisions be made simultaneously. In other words, programmatic initiatives must fit within the "budgetary envelope." If budget ceilings are established early in the development phase it is more likely that the scope of work will realistically conform to budgetary limitations rather than the other way around, which is an invitation to huge cost overruns—and guess who is responsible for those? If cost sharing is required, be very circumspect in how it will be provided. Most organizations typically cost share personnel time and effort; that is, if they are being paid from nongovernmental funds. Don't be afraid to bargain the cost share amounts, particularly after you have been awarded the grant or contract.

Sustainability Plan

I've had to write sustainability plans into numerous budgets and proposals. Interestingly, whether the project operates for one year or ten years, I have never been required to financially continue supporting on-going project activities once the donor funding period has ended. This is not to say it will never happen, but I haven't seen it in over 40 years of working in this arena. The classic responses are: (a) move to a fee for service model; (b) engage new donors, such as local or county governments, particularly if you are delivering services in their geographical areas; or (c) approach foundations and corporations for continuation funding. Other than begging on street corners, I personally wouldn't know what else to do.

CHAPTER 14

Writing the Proposal: How to Start, Where to Begin

I t's time to energize our opportunity searching and writing skills and put words to paper. Where to start? I am sure there are hundreds, if not thousands, of good causes worthy of other people's money. The world is full of bad actors who wantonly kill their own citizens for a host of deranged reasons. Let alone poverty, hunger, crime, violence, environmental degradations of every type and stripe, homelessness, and drug addicted children. Indeed, there is literally no end to the deprivations that people here and all over the globe are experiencing, and yet we are in the modern era, when this stuff should no longer be happening.

Solving these problems, man-made or not, requires a response. We have millions of capable organizations ready to respond to whatever man or nature wants to throw at us. This is an ongoing process. For many, the question is not whether we *want* to be part of the solution, but *how* we can become part of the solution.

A SECOND PAIR OF EYES

Behind every successful proposal writer is a great editor. Whether writing a proposal or a book, you need that second pair of eyes. Editors make authors look good, and I was fortunate in all cases to have superb editors backing me up, challenging me, always asking the right questions and making recommendations from the perspective of the reader (in our case, the reviewers). Think about all the different skill sets that contribute to successful proposals. There is the original idea. That "better way" could come from the endless deliberations of a formally-charged task force, as government typically does when everything else has failed. The lead author may have many attributes—it just might be someone who represents the consensus of the group who can integrate all those competing ideas on a piece of paper and make the words believable, compelling, and above all, achievable.

IT TAKES A TEAM

It takes a team, a very professional, experienced and dedicated team, to prepare a proposal. Oftentimes, team members must work late into the night, night after night, to make sure the proposal gets where it is supposed go, or all that time and effort would be for naught. Writing proposals, while never easy and always challenging, is a learning experience. One that will hopefully pay huge dividends for your organization and the conditions you want to remediate the day you receive this message—"We are pleased to inform you that your proposal, 'titled XXX' has been funded. Congratulations!"

A STEP-BY-STEP GUIDE TO WRITING WINNING PROPOSALS

It's time for me to show you how to successfully achieve your grant-getting goals by providing a step-by-step guide to writing winning proposals. This writing paradigm can be easily adapted to federal, foundation, and corporate funding opportunities.

Step 1: Create an Opportunity Response Team

The priority here should be identifying a team leader who assumes full responsibility for guiding the entire effort from beginning to end. That individual should be an employee or a consultant with deep knowledge of your organization. Next, identify and appoint the proposal development and writing team. The lead person must remain with the team until the proposal has been delivered and received by the donor.

When selecting team members, seek out individuals with knowledge specific to the Request for Proposal. They should have superior writing skills and some familiarity with proposals and grant-getting, if possible. Decide if there is going to be a single proposal writer or a writing team. Each approach, whether a solo or group effort, has positives and negatives. Whether an individual or a group effort, free them up from what they are doing now and train them by bringing in a consultant or by sending them to grant-writing workshops (if there is enough time). The team leader should also be capable of fully assuming lead writer responsibilities; that is, if you have such a gifted writer with the requisite knowledge in your organization. If you cannot identify a staff person with these capabilities, then bring in a consultant or outsource the writing to a capable and qualified organization.

Step 2: Identify a Fundable Idea

Do you have a fundable idea that others will support—with their money? That is the most critical part of any "doing good with other people's money" effort. It's the foundation upon which everything else is built. What is a fundable idea, you might ask? In its simplest form, it is an idea that attracts other people's money because the funder recognizes it as an important and impactful issue requiring resolution. It's truly the test of the grant-giving and -getting marketplace. Donors vote with their dollars. A fundable idea should neither be too grandiose nor too limited. It must be a recognized issue or concern that has serious consequences. Donors want to solve the big problems before they throw money at the smaller ones. The list is almost endless because the world is always evolving with bad things happening, whether man-made or due to nature's fury.

Second, fundable ideas must have advocates, those willing to "beat the bushes" to find both money and answers. The money is needed to get those answers, whether it is finding a cure for a new disease that is quickly spreading, like Zika, or trying to understand what goes on in the mind of terrorists.

Step 3: Build a Constituency

There are literally thousands of causes worthy of other people's money. How do you catch a funder's interest their growing pile of heartfelt requests? Bottom line: it takes a constituency, an active and committed one, to get your better idea to the top of the funding pile. The corollary is, if you do not have a constituency for your cause, funding will not follow.

Step 4: Identify Compatible Funding Opportunities

At most, select and agree upon one or possibly two fundable ideas that would have traction with donors. Depending on the constituency and urgency of the issue, it could be a national, regional, or local effort. Ask yourselves, is this a one-off or a concern important only to you and a few others? Or is this a high-impact problem that you believe your organization has real answers to that can have a significant impact?

Perform a deep review of available funding opportunities focusing on donors who have funded similar types of initiatives in the past. Then determine: (a) if your organization is eligible to submit for this grant opportunity; (b) the potential advantages or disadvantages of competing for this particular funding opportunity; (c) how and why this grant opportunity would ultimately benefit current and future constituents; (d) whether your organization has the necessary infrastructure to support a complex new project; (e) if sufficient cost sharing is available, if required by the donor; (f) whether the organization is capable of accounting for grant funding and expenditures according to the stated requirements of the donor; (g) if current facilities are adequate to house new personnel and service new clients; and (h) if your organization can deliver the goods and achieve the agreed-to outcomes on time and within budget.

Step 5: Shop It Around

Identify potential good-fit sponsors and funders. Shop it around. In other words, you must find an individual, government entity, business, corporation, or foundation to raise their hands and agree to at least consider your better idea, and ultimately, to fund it. You can go door-to-door, like the old-time encyclopedia salesmen, asking for small donations, or you can go hunting for potential sponsors with similar interests. In the world of grant- and contract-giving and -getting, novices quickly end up on the side of the road until they figure out the protocols and how to write winning proposal and compete for other people's money. The smart ones are out there building relationships with potential funders—not continuously hounding them every time they accidentally cross paths and begging for dollars, but rather presenting solutions to significant concerns.

Once you've done enough donor and opportunity searching to identify those with strong interests in your area of focus and expertise, the next step is to write a proposal, because that's how the world of grant- and contract-giving and -getting works.

Step 6: Identify Your Proposal Writing Plan

A successful writing plan must faithfully follow sponsor guidelines. Do not attempt to be creative with the proposal format—donors don't have a sense of humor about these things. Recognize you are dealing with a bureaucracy, which means everyone who wants to play in their backyard must strictly adhere to their expectations, rules, procedures, and values.

Step 7: Concept Generation and Thematic Approach

The Writing and Proposal Development Team creates alternate proposal themes and approaches for implementing the new initiative, managing and integrating the program into the existing organizational infrastructure, and is responsible for achieving all donor outcomes. The team presents its recommendations first to the organization and then to leadership, who will decide what funding opportunities and projects will be pursued.

Step 8: Select Your Proposal Writing Approach

AUTHOR-IN-CHIEF: The author-in-chief model is where one staff member or consultant is assigned to bring all those diverse thoughts and ideas from leadership and staff into a coherent draft proposal. The proposal then typically gets torn apart like lions feasting on a baby wildebeest—which is what you want. There is no easy way to take "groupthink" and turn it into a fundable proposal, but it can be done. It's now the job of the editor(s), who, by being out of the fray, can work their unbiased magic and turn the proposal into a polished document by taking all those disjointed thoughts and reorganizing and formatting them in accordance with donor guidelines.

COLLABORATOR APPROACH: You get better ideas and synergy if you have collaborators, so another approach is to assign at least two writers per module, if you have the staff and all the necessary skill sets.

SINGLE WRITER FOR EACH MODULE APPROACH: The advantage to only having one writer per section is that you know who is doing what and you can make writing assignments based on content knowledge, so no one is left wondering what they should be doing. The disadvantage is that every module will have different flavor, even if you specify word count and use a common style.

HYBRID APPROACH: Hire a professional editor to smooth out the writing style issues, ensuring the document has consistency and that it is coherent and responsive to the funding opportunity and announcement.

CONSULTANTS AS ADVISORS: I was very explicit that it takes a team, a well-organized and dedicated team, to prepare and ultimately write winning proposals. While there is no harm (and even some gain) in bringing "externals" into the process, they should be used for the right reasons with a specific added value in mind. For example, they can be impartial arbiters and integrators of the competing ideas and approaches that arise from groupthink in these types of situations. Or, they can help organize and help plan the proposal process—I am talking about the proposal development process, from start to finish. Remember, it's not finished until you are notified that the proposal and all its accompanying "stuff" now resides in the hands of the intended recipients on time and is deemed compliant for further review.

CONSULTANTS AS OBJECTIVE REVIEWERS: Another area in which consultants can be helpful is as independent reviewers. Using this method, their task is to read and score the proposal through the eyes of reviewers. No punches pulled, because this is your best and last opportunity to clean-up the proposal. A consultant, one that has extensive experience in all phases of proposal writing and development, can provide one last quality check by applying similar scoring standards used by reviewers. In other words, they can determine how that proposal might look to reviewers and how it would stack up against the competition. But now you still have the time to make adjustments that can enhance the document's funding competitiveness. Don't shoot the messenger; listen to them, as hard as it might be to hear what they are telling you—it's better coming from a friendly third-party who has your interests at heart rather than learning your fate from a form letter.

CONSULTANTS AS TEACHERS: Another option is to use consultants as teachers, which immediately brings-to-mind that famous adage, "Give a man a fish and you feed him for a day; teach a man to fish and you feed him for a lifetime." I firmly believe in this proverb. A consultant can coach the team and become a "proposal shepherd," someone who will let team members know when they are going down the wrong path and gently nudge them back on track. Everyone needs a mentor, and I had some great ones.

Step 9: Establish a Countdown Calendar

The countdown calendar is your guide, your best and worst enemy, and your constant companion for the duration. Every action and task on that plan, including a fully complete and sponsor-compliant proposal, must be submission ready at least 10 business days prior to the donor's submission deadline. The countdown calendar begins the day and the hour you give the green light to compete for a grant or contract.

The most critical date on that countdown calendar is the submission date. If your proposal is delivered 5 minutes after that submission date and time, it will be deemed non-compliant. Clearly, you must identify critical dates, including what tasks need to be accomplished within what that time frame and what individual or group is responsible for completing those tasks and hold people accountable to meet the deadlines. The proposal must be finished, package in hand, hopefully with at least a deep review by a professional editor. Lastly, the proposal must be reviewed by the CEO, who must sign the document in several places for it to be deemed compliant.

Step 10: Integrate the "Different Voices" Into a Coherent Proposal

This is probably one of the most important and difficult steps in the process. One individual, your best content writer, must now take a document that is essentially a patchwork of different voices and concepts and create a unified and persuasive proposal-winning document. This is what I call detail work, requiring someone with infinite patience and superb writing skills. It's much like turning scraps of different fabric into an exquisite quilt, which is really a work of art—as your proposal should be.

Step 11: Establish a Budget Building Team

The budget team is a key component in the submission process. This team should be established co-terminus with the writing team. They must remain continuously informed and invited to participate in project design and management meetings so they can estimate costs of doing business, ensuring that the organization doesn't under-budget or over-extend. Their task is to come up with a reasonable project budget that is competitive and consistent with donor funding expectations; one that fairly represents the nonprofit's actual cost of doing business. The team must also scour the program announcement to identify any budget issues that could impact the organization, such as (a) required cost sharing; (b) ability to charge approved indirect rates; (c) maximum funding ceilings; (d) financial reporting requirements; and (d) chargebacks for full-time personnel devoting time and effort to the project. These are only some of the major financial issues to be concerned about.

A Warning! Many newbie organizations, in their desire to win their first grant under-budget to make the proposal more attractive to funders. Should the grant be awarded, the winning organization will quickly discover that the requested funding is not sufficient to cover actual costs of doing business. This can have a downstream impact, which can literally bankrupt the nonprofit or cause a seismic shift in dollars to compensate for the under-funding. This weakens the financial health of the nonprofit and jeopardizes their entire business model. So, don't under-budget!

Step 12: Circulate a Working Draft

Don't even consider using your first draft as the submission document. The working draft is just that—a work in progress. It is a vehicle allowing you to test certain assumptions, approaches, and strategies. The working draft should be as close a facsimile to the final product as humanly possible. Proposals typically go through many iterations and changes. They are often being edited, updated, and tinkered with right up to the last possible moment. If you use a professional editor, which I strongly recommend, make sure they have sufficient time to work their magic.

Step 13: Review and Make Final Revisions

No matter how objective you think you can be, you can never be objective enough. It's time to consider using the services of a reviewer. Don't cheap out (so do not use existing staff or significant others, no matter how qualified you believe them to be). Why? Because they won't want to hurt your feelings, and that would defeat the original purpose of having objective reviewers look at your product (the proposal). The best reviewers are: (1) individuals who have familiarity with the donor you are submitting the proposal to; (2) other successful grant and contract getters and writers; and (3) technical writers who know where to put periods, commas, and semi-colons and how to format and properly organize a technical document such as a proposal. Don't be surprised if you're expected to pay for reviewer services—it's money well-spent. Once having identified the review team, instruct them to literally tear the proposal apart, because it's best done now, before it hits the funder's desk.

Step 14: Proposal Packaged

The next step in the proposal preparation process is getting it submission-ready for delivery to the funder. One more time, make sure all pages, headers, certifications, and representations are present and all requirements have been strictly adhered to. Remember, it's going to experience some rough handling, so make sure papers won't separate in transit and that there are no missing or out-of-order pages. The final product must be pristine. These types of simple mechanical mistakes can doom your proposal, so take extra care that it is properly bound and that everything that is supposed to be in there, is. The Program Announcement typically contains specific submission instructions, down to the type of packaging required, including font sizes and types, number of copies required, cover layouts, headings, number of pages, margins, and the like.

Step 15: Confirm Proposal Delivery

I will tell you that in my over 40 years of writing hundreds of proposals (with an estimated 90% success rate), I've never missed a deadline—but I've come close several times. I learned from my mistakes. While the current delivery systems are lightyears ahead of what I experienced, there are still opportunities to screw up. So as a fall back we would purchase a "two-way airline ticket" and have a trusted staff member standing by to deliver the proposal in person if there was insufficient time to get the proposal to the funder on time through traditional delivery channels. Just a word to the wise!

Step 16: Congratulate Yourselves

Congratulations, you've accomplished your goal, met all your deadlines, and submitted a competitive proposal to the donor. You all should be very proud of yourself. Now, high-fives for all, go home get some sleep. Win or lose, you're in the game because you now know that collaboration works, and more importantly, you're a team that has the right stuff.

CHAPTER 15

Looking Behind the Curtain: How Proposals are Ranked and Selected for Funding

IT'S JUDGEMENT TIME

Reviews can take many forms, depending on who is doing the reviewing and selecting. The reviews and the reviewers have one thing in common: they need to make funding judgements, and the more informed the judgement, the fairer the process will be. I am using a review and selection paradigm that reflects many of the selection criteria proposal review teams use to rank, and then select, which proposals are funded and which are not.

Submitted proposals are first reviewed for technical compliance with the RFP (Request for Proposal). For example, criteria might include: Is the submitting organization eligible and/or qualified to receive funding under the provisions of this specific RFP? Do they have appropriate documentation, such as proof of nonprofit status and the execution of all appropriate certifications and representations? Do they have any prior sanctions, negative audits, incomplete progress reports, or failure to adequately document claimed outcomes and accomplishments related to previously funded activities? Is the technical proposal complete and in full compliance with the RFP?

The proposals making it through that first review filter are then moved on to program review, or "technical evaluation." Reviews in this phase are often conducted by in-house staff members, and sometimes the donor enhances these teams with external program experts and community representatives. Reviewers independently score each proposal. After all the proposals have been reviewed, the team meets to discuss their assigned scores and go through how they arrived at those scores. Proposals are then separated into a sort of "pass/fail" system, where those above the line are moved to a final round evaluation for further review and consideration. Here, reviewers again typically meet as a team and attempt to come to a consensus as to which proposals are fundable and which are not fundable under the provisions of this specific program announcement. Depending on the organization and their specific evaluation protocols, the review team's work is over.

HOW PROPOSALS ARE SCORED

There are other types of review protocols. Some rank proposals from high to low; based on your position on the list and available funding, you are either funded or not. Federal agencies almost always conduct a second review which focuses on the budget: how realistic it is and whether it is "too rich" or "too thin." Either could knock the proposal out of funding contention or trigger a meeting with the submitting organization, at which time financial details are worked out or not. If the sponsor believes the financials are unrealistic, they will move the proposal down the list and move a lower-cost compliant proposal up the list. Over the years, I had been involved in numerous grant and contract negotiations where funders would ask questions and ask for clarifications. Most of those questions focused on work plans and outcomes, as well as budgetary issues. Sometimes, when proposals appear to be equally scored and compliant, the sponsor can ask for a "best and final" from those submitters. That means each organization selected for the best and final will have one more opportunity to reduce the cost proposal and/or enhance their outcomes and deliverables.

Proposals are either funded or not based on their relative ratings and rankings compared against series-proscribed criteria. Because of that, it would be informative to "look behind the scoring curtain" by becoming familiar with the rating criteria reviewers use to select which proposals, whether grants or contracts, will be funded and which will not. This can educate and refocus future proposal writing approaches and strategies—provided, of course, you integrate this new knowledge into your proposal writing strategies. This is my version of the type of review both grants and contracts are subjected to, based on my 40 years of writing winning proposals.

Technical Compliance and Eligibility Check List

- Eligible Applicant   Yes ☐   No ☐

- Compliant Proposal   Yes ☐   No ☐

- Required Certifications   Yes ☐   No ☐

- Submitted within Deadline Yes ☐   No ☐

A "no" designation on any of these criteria means the proposal will be removed from consideration and deemed non-compliant.

PROPOSAL RATING CRITERIA

Scoring: Use a 1-10 scale, with 1 being the lowest score and with 5 being the mid- or neutral point.

I. Significance of Problem
- Does the proposal address a priority concern or significant problem? Does it identify associated contributing factors and the magnitude and the criticality of the problem? Is it responsive to the RFP?   _____

- Is there sufficient data and information to demonstrate the purported importance and magnitude of the problem or need?   _____

- Does the proposal clearly identify proposed goals, objectives, and outcomes? Are these consistent with and capable of addressing the problem and attaining project objectives and outcomes?   _____

- Are the applicants aware of previous attempts and actions taken to resolve this problem or meet identified needs?   _____

II. Potential Impact of Proposed Project
- How many people/institutions will be positively impacted by this proposed project?   _____

- What is the prospect for lasting or long-term structural change and improvement?   _____

- Are identified procedures and benchmarks in place to review and assess ongoing progress?   _____

- Can successes be replicated in other communities?   _____

- Does the applicant clearly identify the potential barriers to successful implementation and how they can be preemptively addressed? _____

- Does the applicant demonstrate the ability to quickly pivot and change their model if results are less than satisfactory? _____

- Will applicant's efforts inform others and become a benchmark for how to resolve this type and class of problem in other communities? _____

- Will the community be informed and/or involved in the resolution of the identified problem? _____

- Does applicant demonstrate the capacity to objectively evaluate project success and outcomes? _____

III. Work Plan and Management Approach
- Does the applicant have a documented record of success in managing projects with similar complexity and requirements? _____

- Does the applicant demonstrate the capability and capacity for resolving or significantly impacting the identified need or problem? _____

- Does the applicant clearly indicate the tasks to be accomplished and the sequence of activities which must occur? _____

- Does the applicant have the appropriate in-house mix of human assets, resources, and technology to impact the identified problem? _____

- Is the work plan consistent with the complexity of the problem? _____

- Are program plans, work tasks, and schedules clearly stated? _____

- Are objectives, deliverables, and outcomes identified and measurable?   _____

- Are key personnel identified and assigned to appropriate tasks with appropriate time commitments? Is there a clear delineation and accountability for their distribution of time and effort?   _____

- Has the applicant conducted a cost/benefit analysis to demonstrate savings resulting from program?   _____

IV. Qualifications
- Has the applicant demonstrated the requisite organizational and delivery infrastructure, leadership capacity, and experience to successfully prosecute and deliver identified outcomes and deliverables?   _____

- Does the applicant assume and recognize their responsibility for project completion on time and within budget?   _____

- Are staff qualified by education, training, and experience in project-related fields?   _____

- Is there an appropriate mix of skills and expertise, and do they complement each other?   _____

- Does the applicant value and maintain positive relationships with other nonprofits, government officials and community members?   _____

V. Budget Plan
- Is the budget reasonable and appropriate given the reach, complexity, and potential project outcomes?   _____

- If not, does it appear to be too high or too low given the proposed deliverables and outcomes?   _____

PROPOSAL RATING CRITERIA

- Are all budgeted items necessary and essential to achieve program deliverables and outcomes? _____

- Are costs well-documented? Will donor funds be expended and accounted for separately from other funding sources? _____

- Does the applicant have an approved indirect rate? _____

- If cost-sharing is required, does the applicant demonstrate the capacity to provide required cost-sharing? _____

Summary Rating Sheet

Proposal Title: _____

Submitting Organization: _____

ID# : _____

Proposal Title: _____

Reviewer: _____

Significance of Problem: _____ / _____/ _____/

Impact: _____ / _____/ _____/

Work Plan: _____ / _____/ _____/

Qualifications: _____ / _____/ _____/

Budget: _____ / _____/ _____/

Totals: _____ / _____/ _____/

Final Average Score: _____

THE AWARD ANNOUNCEMENT: WHAT YOU'VE ALL BEEN WAITING FOR

Now that you have officially submitted your proposal, you can sit back and wait, wait some more, and wait some more again. But believe it or not, there is a lot of activity going on behind that curtain. Some review protocols might be informal, while others might be highly structured, going through a labyrinth of reviews and using a scoring system that can take weeks, or even months, to come out the other side with a decision. Most donors, public and private, have a reputation for fairness to protect and take their decisions very seriously, requiring highly structured review and selection processes.

The power to award funding resides in the hands of a relatively few individuals. In foundations, the decision might fall to senior staff members, program experts, board members, family members, or community members. Corporate funding decisions, depending on the award size, might reside with local or regional corporate officers, marketing staff, and/or community members. If the funder is a corporate foundation, reviews are typically conducted by a combination of foundation staff and officials, invited external reviewers, and content experts. Some might use a two-tiered approach using a combination of community residents, content specialists, and corporate officials to make the decision of who gets the funding and who gets the "thank you for applying" letter. Once funding decisions are finalized, the awardees are notified. Don't get too relaxed just yet there is a lot more legal, technical, and bureaucratic stuff you must deal with before the dollars flow.

Notice of Award

Federal grantors issue a Notice of Grant Award (NGA) for each application selected for funding. The NGA stipulates: (a) project and budget period; (b) amount of federal assistance; (c) terms and conditions of award; and (d) financial and programmatic reporting requirements. The Agency's Grant Manager of record provides: (a) prior approvals when required; (b) reviews Indirect Cost Agreements; (c) responds to Freedom of Information Act requests; (d) issues notices of suspensions/termination; and (e) continuously monitors fiscal management to ensure fiscal/program integrity. Above all, don't let your success blind you to the flood of requirements and the new responsibilities that comes along with the money, together with any special terms, requirements, or conditions that might apply to your award.

Oh, and you're going to have new best friends, also known as your very own Program Officer and Grant Management Specialist, who have joint responsibility for overseeing your project. Their objective is to help smooth out the rough edges and educate you about all those interesting new reports you will be submitting throughout the entire funding period. If you get an understanding Program Officer, they can be very helpful in translating all those new requirements, becoming your advocate rather than your worst nightmare; provided you are up front with them and let them know when you encounter problems, rather than sweeping them under the rug.

CHAPTER 16

You Won the Grant or Contract So Now What?

READ BEFORE YOU SIGN

Once you have been officially notified that your proposal was accepted for funding, your first conscious act should be to congratulate each other, and the second should be to read the award notice. Signing the agreement is not just a formality or a one-way negotiation. Rather, it is you committing your organization to all those terms and conditions contained in the formal agreement.

But hold on, it's not as simple as it might appear. Awards made by foundations and corporations can be relatively straightforward, most of the time. Federally funded awards, particularly contracts, are much more complex, because you are dealing with the most complex bureaucracy on Planet Earth. You will be expected to execute either grant or contract terms and conditions. It's advisable to have an attorney familiar with these matters to review the award notice and provide wise counsel. You can negotiate award terms and conditions to a point. Some nonprofits, particularly those that routinely deal with grants and contracts, are intimately familiar with typical grant and contract provisions and have already established sophisticated administrative mechanisms to deal with these numerous regulations.

A word to the wise from someone who's been there and done that: unfortunately, the less experienced or first-time grant and contract winners are not typically fluent in "grantese." They can be shocked into stunned silence when first encountering the labyrinth of grant and contract provisions. However, if you want to be competitive in the grant space, you must be prepared to operate under their rules, not yours! Here are some general suggestions on how to get along with your new best friends and funders—those who hold your fate in their hands, whether government, foundations, or corporations.

HOW TO GET ALONG WITH YOUR FUNDERS

RULE # 1: Always keep your funder's representatives happy and on your side, because they are the ones standing between you and the "bureaucrats." Whether you like it or not, you now have a partner. The relationship can become one of mutual support and trust or deteriorate into a constant state of tension and conflict—your choice.

RULE # 2: Treat your sponsoring organization as you would have them treat you. Roads go both ways. If you are constantly complaining about terms, conditions, or payments, chances are the sponsor will throw it back at you. Sponsors or funders are used to calling the shots, while awardees are imbued with a naïve faith in their own abilities. Whenever possible, try not to widen the gap over inconsequential matters; rather, do things that bring you together.

RULE # 3: Never use a grant or contract for personal gain or advancement. Nothing dampens enthusiasm for your project quicker than the perception that you are using it as a stepping stone to bigger and better things (or for personal benefit). So, if you have money in the budget for a conference, it should be directly related to the success of your project, not because it is scheduled for Hawaii. (You get my point)

RULE #4: Make sure you have all the necessary administrative and technological infrastructure in place as well as the individuals who know how to use them. Your project will be financially audited! No excuses like you lost the receipts, or, *oh, we didn't know we violated the salary* *cap.* This is the quickest way to get your project shut down and earn the reputation of a "gamer," not an "honest dealer."

RULE #5: Whatever outcomes and deliverables you agreed to achieve, make sure that you remain on time and within budget. You signed an agreement, so ditch the excuses and get down to business; that means not only saying what you will do, but even more importantly, doing what you say.

RULE #6: Learn their language; don't expect them to learn yours. I call it "grantese," the official language of grant- and contract-getting. Understanding this language enables you to: (a) communicate with federal donors; (b) understand and analyze Requests for Proposals; (c) select best fit opportunities; (d) develop a working knowledge of grant terms and conditions so you can intelligently respond to funding opportunities; and (e) once funded, can administer the grant or contract.

GRANTESE: GRANT AND CONTRACT TERMS YOU NEED TO KNOW!

Without at least a familiarity and fluency with this new language, you won't know what you are applying for or obligating your organization to comply with. You will need, at the very least, a working knowledge of some basic grant terms to be competitive in the world of grant- and contract-winning and -getting. Consider this your first language lesson!

AWARD: Financial assistance that provides support or stimulation to accomplish a public purpose. Awards include grants, contracts, and other agreements in the form of money by the federal government to an eligible recipient to carry out a federal program. The term "award" can be used to generically refer to grants, contracts, and cooperative agreements. This what you are competing for: an AWARD!

COST-SHARING: Now we come to perhaps the most misunderstood concept faced by "first-timers." Many funders expect the recipients of their largess to have some skin in the game, and this is "cost sharing;" the portion of project costs not borne by the funding agency or the federal government. The ultimate responsibility for providing required cost-sharing rests squarely on the shoulder of the primary awardee (that's you). Cost-sharing can either be in real dollars or in-kind services, such as time and effort of staff devoted to the project who are not paid from the project, and it also can refer to equipment and/or facilities. Those things ultimately equal, in real-dollar terms, a share or the total agreed-to cost sharing requirement.

MAINTENANCE OF EFFORT: A federal grant recipient is required to maintain a specified base of continued financial effort and not supplant those funds with federal grant dollars.

APPLICATION PACKAGE: A group of specific forms and documents for a specific funding opportunity

PROJECT COSTS: Total allowable costs incurred under a federal award and all required cost-sharing, including third party contributions.

RECIPIENT: A non- federal entity that receives a federal award directly from a federal awarding agency to carry out an activity under a federal program. The term "recipient" does not include sub-recipients.

SUB-RECIPIENT: A non-federal entity that receives a sub-award from a pass-through entity.

ELIGIBILITY: The status an entity must possess to be considered for an award, as specified by authorizing legislation and programmatic regulations. Generally, eligible entities are public and nonprofit private organizations and institutions, including faith-based and community-based organizations, state/local governments and their agencies, and federally recognized Indian tribes or tribal organizations. For-profit organizations are eligible to receive awards under financial assistance programs when authorized.

SOUL SOURCE AGREEMENTS: Federal agencies and state entities using federally-sourced funds are permitted to issue sole source agreements, which means the donor can select an eligible organization without an open competition, for three primary reasons: (a) the singular and unique capacities and capabilities required; (b) time-sensitive project or procurement; and (c) secrecy and national security.

LETTER OF INTENT: To help in planning the application review process, some programs request a letter of intent from the applicant in advance of the application deadline. These are neither binding nor mandatory.

PROJECT PERIOD: The total time for which support of a discretionary project has been programmatically approved. The project period usually consists of a series of budget periods of a one-year duration.

THE PRE-AWARD PROCESS: Federal Contract and Program Officers are restricted as to what information and support they can provide to non-profit organizations before the proposal has been submitted and during the entire review process. That's for the right reasons. They can, however, provide information that is publicly available in federal and government documents, including: (a) information and clarification of requirements regarding procedures, eligibility, and proposal submissions; (b) grant management policies and requirements; (c) general information in regard to programmatic issues; and (e) general information regarding evaluation criteria and reporting requirements.

THE POST-AWARD PROCESS: The Post-Award Period begins the day you receive your NGA, or Notice of Grant Award. Your award letter will identify your Project Period, or when project funding begins and when it will end. Your cognizant agency (the agency that funded you) is now allowed to communicate with you and your organization, something it could not do during the proposal review process. Your Program Officer can assist you and answer any questions regarding the award and how to move forward without tangling yourself up in a lot of red tape. The Program or the Grants Officer can also: (a) provide more specific and project-related advice and clarity on budget and management concerns; (b) explain the agency's grants management policies; (c) assist with any federal regulations that you are expected to comply with; (d) describe your nonprofit's reporting obligations and the agency's evaluation requirements; and, (e) acquaint you with the dreaded compliance and financial audits you are required to perform and provide to the donor organization. Besides helping, they're also watching; that is, making sure you are following all federal requirements, and believe me, there are lots of them. The Grant Manager can review and approve requests for prior approvals when required. They will review Indirect Cost Agreements for compliance with donor policies, respond to freedom of information requests, and continuously monitor program progress and fiscal management to ensure fiscal/program integrity as well as compliance with all OMB (Office of Management and Budget Circulars) bulletins and circulars is met. Most monitoring takes the form of required self-reporting, of which there will be a lot.

INDIRECT COSTS AND DIRECT COSTS: Federal grants involve two types of costs: direct and indirect. Direct costs are those that are allocated to project activities, like personnel, travel, equipment, and contracted services. So, if you purchase a computer to support the project and it ends up in your house (because you reasoned you can work from home) that would be an "audit exception." Or if a project employee, who is paid from project funds, also runs errands for the Director on project time, you are once again failing to properly allocate project funds. In addition, and very importantly, you cannot use federal funds to supplant or replace nonprofit funds if they are not directly project related.

Indirect costs are more difficult to cleanly identify and allocate (hence being called "indirect"). Indirect costs are typically related to facilities and administration. Knowledgeable nonprofits typically negotiate their Indirect Rates with their cognizant or assigned federal agency, rather than settle for the default rate of 10%. Whatever rate you negotiate or accept now applies to current and future federally-sponsored activities and grants awarded to your organization. Indirect rates are typically represented as a percentage of total expended grant direct costs. The funding agency will review and verify any indirect costs charged and/or the establishment of an indirect cost rate—this is a good thing. They will provide information to grantees without approved indirect rates on how to negotiate and establish a federally-approved indirect cost rate for their organizations. The default rate, until an indirect cost rate is established and approved, is typically 10% of salaries/wages. In other words, if you spend $50,000 a month on salaries, you can retain 10% of that amount, or $5,000, to support the costs associated with operating the federal grant.

RECORDS RETENTION: The recipient (that's you) must retain all required records, become instantly familiar with all that federal regulatory stuff contained in the (OMB) Office of Management and Budget circulars, and make sure the organization is fully compliant with regulatory and accounting requirements of the federal sponsor. Remember, all those certifications and representations you signed, but probably did not read or understand? Regardless, you are now responsible for compliance with all those as well. Welcome to the wonderful world of federal grants!

BUDGET MONITORING: The Awardee is required to monitor and adhere to program guidance pertaining to budget requirements; whether costs were allowable or unallowable based on the budget as approved in the grant award. In other words, there is an extensive list of "unallowable costs" (so get to know them), otherwise, you will be writing one big check sometime in the future when the final audit identifies all those "unallowable costs." Take this issue seriously, because if you are profligate with government monies, you can't ever expect to receive another grant.

SITE VISITS: Awarding agencies can make invited or uninvited site visits. This provides an opportunity for federal staff to meet with grant project teams and view the project in action. Site visit teams can consist of program staff, federal grant management staff, and technical assistance consultants.

SITE VISITS FINANCIAL MANAGEMENT SYSTEMS: All federal grantees are required to have approved financial management systems that are fully capable of providing timely, accurate, current, and complete disclosure of financial information while providing oversight and protection of Federal funds. Consistent with OMB Circular A-133.

SITE VISITS OTHER RECORDS: Project records that verify programmatic participation, services delivered, and client participation, as well as personnel- and HR-related policies and procedures. In addition, procurement policies and procedures and any other basic administrative regulations that have a bearing on the project being funded by the award can be reviewed or audited at any time!

REPORTING REQUIREMENTS: Progress Reporting: Grantees are required to submit periodic reports to reflect the progress on activities-to-date based on the outcomes and deliverables that you identified in the proposal. The Notice of Grant Award (NGA) identifies the frequency and information to be included in these reports; FFR (Federal Financial Reports) are due 90 days after the budget period ends and provides the details of the grantees spending for that period.

Federal Cost Principles

All grantees are monitored to ensure adherence to all program, budget, and project requirements. This includes adherence to appropriate federal administrative and financial requirements and other budget requirements, including allocability and reasonality, of costs consistent with appropriate OMB bulletins. I know, it doesn't make a lot of sense, but it's here that many nonprofits go off the tracks. That is, they lose track of the money, and when that happens the roof caves in. These rules are used to achieve uniformity in the treatment of costs by specific types of recipient organizations including: educational institutions, state governments, local governments, nonprofits, and Indian tribes. Get seriously familiar with these Office of Management and Budget Circulars (OMBs) because more likely than not, they will be applied to your organization.

CIRCULAR A-21: Cost Principles for Educational Institutions: Circular A-21 is applicable to research and development, training, and other sponsored work performed by colleges and universities under grants, contracts, and other agreements.

CIRCULAR A-110: Uniform Administrative Requirements for Grants and Other Agreements with Institutions of higher education, hospitals, and other nonprofit organizations.

CIRCULAR A-133: Accounting standards for obtaining consistency and uniformity among federal agencies for the audit of states, local governments, and nonprofit organizations expending federal awards.

AUDIT REQUIREMENTS: Annual Audits: All grantees must have an audit performed in accordance with OMB Circular A-133 for fiscal years where federal expenditures were greater than $500,000.

OUR LANGUAGE LESSON IS JUST BEGINNING

It's time to dive in with both feet. Yes, your head will spin, but if you want to compete for and administer federal funding, it must be done. The following is the unexpurgated version of how our federal government defines various funding vehicles.

Award Types

The federal government and its agencies have three primary vehicles for awarding funds to nonprofits and those are grants, contracts, and cooperative agreements. These are considered *competed awards*; that is, others are also seeking or applying for these funding opportunities.

Please pay close attention to the new vocabulary you must learn if you are to become grant-getters!

There are several different types of grants and grant opportunities; some are available to nonprofits, while others are restricted to units of government, including tribal governments. Grants and contracts share certain similarities, such as both must be authorized by law and both are subject to available appropriations. Grants and contracts are publicly announced and eligible organizations are encouraged to respond. Both types of opportunities are awarded on a competitive basis, through objective assessment of disinterested third parties. They diverge because each are governed by differing regulations, terms, and conditions and purpose of the activity.

GRANTS: A federal grant is a monetary award of financial assistance given to a recipient to carry out some work for a charitable public purpose for the public good. The grantee has certain requirements and obligations that, if not fulfilled as expected, will lead to possible legal repercussions. Federal grants are awarded to state and county governments or to nonprofit agencies who have been designated as 501(c)(3) tax-exempt organizations under the Internal Revenue Service.[1]

CONTRACTS: These vehicles are used when the purpose of the activity is to provide goods or services directly to the federal government in support of its public mission and purpose. Grants are the vehicle of choice if the principle use is to advance a congressionally authorized action for a defined public or private purpose in which services are not rendered to the federal government. The Federal Grant and Cooperative Agreement Act of 1977 provides a standardized test to determine whether to award a grant or a contract, called the Benefit or Use Test. Contracts are different types of award agreements; not better or worse than grants or cooperative agreements, just different and used for different purposes. It's a procurement, which means government is buying something. That

---

1   www.federalgrants.com/what-is-a-grant.html

"something" could be a product or a service and there are different procedures for selecting providers of products and services (31 USC 6303).

COOPERATIVE AGREEMENTS: When an awarding agency expects to be substantially involved in a project, the law requires use of a cooperative agreement. A cooperative agreement is much like a grant in that the process is about the same, but how it is managed and how decisions are made relative to operating these types of agreements are shared between the awarded organization and the federal agency who issued the award.

TYPES OF GRANTS AVAILABLE TO NONPROFITS AND FAITH-BASED ORGANIZATIONS

PROJECT GRANTS: These types of grants are what nonprofits are most familiar with and typically compete for. This is the most-used vehicle for moving federal dollars to nonprofits. Project grants keep the Feds in the driver's seat, exercising almost total control of the program, process, and money. Federal funding agencies unilaterally decide: (a) what qualifications the submitting nonprofits must have to compete for project funding; (b) what outcomes and deliverables must be achieved; (c) what populations can benefit from these funds; and (d) project time frame, funding cycle, and reimbursement schedule. And, of course, politics doesn't end up in the equation. I competed for, and received, hundreds of project grants over three decades, and some are still being funded today. My best guess is that my team and I won some $500 million dollars in federal awards. I know what it takes to apply for and win grants.[2]

DISCRETIONARY GRANTS: A grant or cooperative agreement for which a federal awarding agency may select the recipient from among all eligible applicants and may or may not decide to make an award based

---

2   Congress of the United States Congressional Budget Office, CBO, March 2013

on programmatic, technical, or scientific content of an application and can decide the amount of funding to be awarded.

CONTINUATION GRANT: An extension or renewal of an existing program providing funding for one or more additional funding periods that would otherwise expire. This is a very good thing to have happen.

GRANTS AVAILABLE TO STATES, UNITS OF GOVERNMENT, TRIBAL AND TERRITORIAL GOVERNMENTS

MANDATORY GRANT PROGRAMS: Mandatory grants are just that; grants that federal agencies are required to award by statute to state, tribal, and territorial governments. These types of grants comprise 80% of the Administration for Children and Families' (ACF) grant portfolio. The remaining 20% is awarded through discretionary grant processes to a variety of organizations, including states, localities, tribal, and territorial governments, academic institutions, and nonprofits, including community and faith-based organizations that support ACF's mission.[3]

CATEGORICAL FORMULA GRANTS: These types of grants are typically awarded to qualifying states and local entities and are either congressionally legislated or administratively determined. For example, Title I Funds, which provide significant educational funding to states for disadvantaged children and families, allow state and local educational entities to set education and use policies but require outcome data to demonstrate continuing progress against agreed-to outcomes and deliverables. Medicaid is another program that allows states to customize the delivery of Medicaid-funded benefits to populations to meet specific needs and circumstances. States have come up with surprisingly good approaches that saved money, reduced inefficiencies (sometimes called fraud), and provided enhanced services to eligible participants.

---

3   www.acf.hhs.gov/grants

INTERGOVERNMENTAL GRANTS: Intergovernmental grants are formula-funded federal funds that flow to states and localities. The federal government, as represented by its departments and agencies, attaches conditions and pre-determines how recipient entities can spend these funds—so much for intergovernmental collaboration. These are typically categorized as Block Grants, Categorical Formula Grants, or Project Grants. Each differs in the amount of control the federal government can require over how state and local governments spend these monies.

BLOCK GRANTS: Block grants give state and local governments greater flexibility and control over how funds are expended; that's why our trusting federal government doesn't use this vehicle very often. Heaven forbid, they should be used in new and innovative ways not approved of by the political flavor of the day. According to the Urban Institute, "Congress has eroded the flexibility of Block Grants by adding restrictions, requiring state and local government cost-sharing or by creating new categorical programs to replace the more flexible block grants."[4]

---

4   The Urban Institute, Government-Nonprofit Contracting Relationships, Brief #1, May 2013

SOME FINAL WORDS

We've come a long way together. I did my best to demystify all that government, foundation, and corporate "grant and contract speak" by providing integrated, step-by-step strategies, processes, and progressions, allowing nonprofit, faith-based organizations, schools, colleges and universities to make their neighborhoods, communities, cities, towns, nation and world a better place for all to live. How? By successfully competing for and winning grants, contracts, and awards from government, corporations, and foundations.

Ultimately, it's not about how much money we win, but about what we do with those very precious dollars. It's about helping our children and our schools; it's about preserving our planet for future generations; it's about children having children and stopping inter-generational poverty; it's about hunger and violence; it's about making our neighborhoods, our communities our nation, and our world a better place for all; it's about coming together in common cause, not about we won and you lost. This is your opportunity to re-energize your nonprofit, faith-based organization, school, or college by becoming part of the "global solution", not turning a blind eye to the "manmade misery" that daily impacts life on planet earth. The "pen," in this case, is truly mightier than the sword—so write that proposal and above all,

ENJOY the RIDE!